Feel like no one's
someone who al
and even better-

GET WITH GOD

LYNN H. PRYOR

BROADMAN
&HOLMAN
PUBLISHERS

Nashville, Tennessee

Printed in the United States of America

Published by:
Broadman & Holman Publishers
Nashville, Tennessee

Designed by:
Steven Boyd

4261-61
0-8054-6161-2

Dewey Decimal Classification: 248.32
Subject Heading: Prayer \ Teenagers—Religious Life
Library of Congress Card Catalog Number: 94-39205

Unless otherwise noted, all Scripture quotations are from the Holy
Bible, New International Version, copyright © 1973, 1978, 1984 by
International Bible Society; used by permission of Zondervan
Publishing House.
    "He Paid a Debt" printed with permission from Soro Publishing,
Dallas, Texas. "One Solitary Life," author unknown, is reprinted on
page 22 of this book.

Library of Congress Cataloging-in-Publication Data
Pryor, Lynn H., 1958–
    Get with God / Lynn H. Pryor
        p. cm.
    ISBN 0-8054-6161-2
    1. Prayer—Christianity—Juvenile literature. 2. Lord's
prayer—Juvenile literature. 3. Prayer—Christianity—Study and
teaching. 4. Lord's prayer—Study and teaching. [1. Prayer.
2. Lord's prayer. 3. Christian life.] I. Title.
    BV212.P79   1995
    248.3'2—dc20
    94-39205
    CIP

Contents

▼

To
the youth of
Colonial Hill Baptist Church
Snyder, Texas
▼

P R E F A C E

Get Ready for a Great Adventure

▼

Praying can—and should—be a great adventure. Linking arms with God and joining Him in His awesome work is an incredible and exciting opportunity.

This book can be a great adventure, too. It is not meant to be just about the great adventure of prayer; this book is meant to be an adventure in itself. It is not meant to be read through in one sitting (even if you do need something to read during a long wait at the orthodontist's office or a long trip through Nebraska). This book is meant to be worked through.

Sure, you can just sit and read it. You'll get a lot of good stuff from it. But to really benefit from this book, try the following:

▼ Read one chapter a day (or one chapter a week). Each chapter closes with a section called "ACTS: Responding to What I Read." In this section, you will be shown some simple, practical ways to pray. These prayers will be based on the things you just learned in that chapter. I urge you to put the book down at that time and pray through these simple suggestions. ACTS is an acronym for prayer:

Adoration—Praising God for who He is
Confession—Admitting to God our sins
Thanksgiving—Thanking God for what He has done
Supplication—Asking God for His help

Use this section as a guide for your prayers that day (or that week). Practice for a day (or for a week) the principles of prayer you learn in one chapter before you move on to the next chapter.

▼ Set aside a certain time and place for your study of prayer. Have some quiet time by yourself so that you can pray as you read.

▼ Study the book with others. Study the chapters with a friend or in a small group. Agree on a meeting time and place. Read one chapter a week, then come together to discuss it and pray together.

Is this just a book to read or an adventure in prayer? The choice is yours!

▼

The Secret

▼

John was still awake. It was not the usual night noises that kept John awake. No cricket chirps. No animal noises. It was an unusually quiet night. What kept him awake was something he had heard that afternoon. It was not the first time he had heard it either. But *this* time, the words took on a new meaning. It was as if he had heard them for the first time.

John shifted his weight on the hay and looked out the open window. Someone else in the room turned over and mumbled briefly in his sleep, but John was too preoccupied to try to figure out who it was. He was thinking about the adventure—there was no other word for it—he had been on the past few years. He was only seventeen, almost eighteen; but, oh, the things that he had seen.

It began when he was fifteen. That's when he first saw Jesus. John and his older brother, James, worked with their father in the family fishing business. Lately, however, they had been spending all their free time following and listening to another John, the one that baptized people. His teaching had a ring of truth and sincerity to it, something the younger John didn't sense in the religious leaders. The younger John began to follow this preacher around, hanging on his every word. So he didn't take it lightly when the older John pointed to Jesus and said *this* is the One to follow and listen to.

So he did. John and his brother decided to devote all their time to following Jesus of Nazareth. In almost three year's time, John had seen and experienced more than other young men even dream about. John had been saved from certain death when he heard Jesus command a storm to stop. He had seen Jesus feed thousands with a lunch that was meant for one young boy. He was there when Jesus took broken people and instantly made them whole again. It hadn't been long since Jesus changed before his eyes on a mountaintop and talked with Moses and Elijah. Could he explain it? No, but the words and teaching of Jesus backed it up: Jesus was different from any other teacher or prophet. No, Jesus wasn't just *different*. He was the Son of God. John knew it.

> For the first time, it hit John: "Jesus wants me to be like Him!"

And that's what made the words John heard that afternoon even more amazing. As they walked along the road into Capernaum, Jesus taught his close circle of twelve disciples and answered their questions. Jesus reminded the twelve that anyone who trusted Him would do the things He was doing. That hit John hard, and he began to connect it with other things he had heard Jesus say time and again. For the first time, it hit John: *Jesus wants me to be like Him!*

John was both excited at the invitation and confused about the reality of it. *How can I be like Jesus?* John thought. *Jesus is the Son of God, but if He wants me to be like Him, there must be a secret. But what? What can I learn from Jesus that will make me like Him? Should I ask Jesus to teach me how to preach to the crowds? Should I ask Jesus to teach me where to get His wisdom so that I can answer any question like He does? Maybe Jesus could show me how to turn water into wine.*

John turned over and nudged his brother James with his foot. "Psst, James." John found James's rib cage with his big toe and nudged him again. "Psst, James," he whispered again.

James turned over and opened his eyes to the shadows and darkness around him. "Hmm?" he said sleepily.

John leaned toward his brother. "James, Jesus wants us to be like Him, doesn't He?"

"Hmmm," James responded. John could see his brother nodding his head in the shadows.

"How?"

"How what?" James asked, expressing a little irritation at being woken up by his younger brother.

"What's the catch? How in the world can we be like Jesus?"

James stared for a moment, still half-asleep. He was not in a frame of mind for thinking. "I don't know."

"Well, *I* want to know."

"What do you want me to say, John?" James paused. "Just pray about it. It'll come to you." With that, he rolled over and went back to sleep.

Profound answer, big brother, John thought, *Pray about it.* Then, for the second time that day, John had a flash of insight. *That's it! Pray about it. I've seen Jesus do all sorts of miracles in all sorts of ways, but the one thing I've seen Jesus do consistently is pray!*

John tossed on the pallet of hay again. He didn't have a complete answer, but he knew what he was going to do. He had heard Jesus talk about prayer before, but John wanted to hear Him talk about it again. This time John would be listening with a greater intensity. John finally drifted off to sleep rehearsing the question he would ask Jesus in the morning: "Master, teach me to pray."

▼

PART ONE

Asking the Right Questions

▼

So you want to learn to pray? You're in the right place! This book will teach you about prayer by taking you back to where the disciples learned about prayer—to Jesus.

When the disciples said, "Lord, teach us to pray," Jesus taught them a model prayer (found in Matthew 6:9–13). This prayer is commonly called the Lord's Prayer, but a better title would be the Model Prayer. This model shows us the types of things about which we should pray.

Jesus did more than just teach His disciples what to pray. By His lifestyle, Jesus taught them how to pray. Let's see how—and why—Jesus prayed.

If Jesus was God, why did He need to pray?

What sort of things did Jesus pray about?

What is God like? Who exactly am I talking to?

We should begin, though, with the most important question of all:

Is prayer really necessary?

O N E

Why Bother?

*Your Father knows what you need
before you ask him.*

Matthew 6:8

▼

The dreaded day had arrived. Final exams. Dennis slammed his locker shut, took a deep breath, and made his way down the hall to Mr. Curry's classroom. Dennis was nervous, yet confident. An *A* on the science final would give Dennis a passing grade and allow him to graduate in eight days.

The test was placed on his desk face-down. On the other side of that white paper was the key to his graduation. Dennis tried to shake his nervousness. *I've studied. I'm prepared. I know this stuff.*

At Mr. Curry's signal, Dennis turned over the exam. He quickly wrote his name at the top (points deducted, you know, if there's no name at the top) and read the first question: "How far is Jupiter from the sun? Answer must be accurate within one inch." *Within one inch?!* thought Dennis, *I haven't got a clue.*

Dennis stared at the second question: "How many species of insects are there on the island of Borneo and exactly how many insects are there in each species?"

Sweat began forming on his forehead. Dennis skipped to the third question: "What is the depth of the Pacific Ocean at 48° 30′ longitude and 163° 42′ latitude?" Dennis began to panic. He said to himself, *Only God knows the answer to these questions.* He put his head on his desk and began to feel sick.

Dennis woke with a start when his head thudded against the tabletop. He looked around at the familiar surroundings: the kitchen table, a long-since-emptied Coke can, and his companion for the last two nights, his science textbook. He shook off the feeling of impending doom and got up to get another soft drink. He was determined to lick that test.

> If God knows everything and He knows what I'm going to say to Him before I say it, then why say it?

Only God Knows . . .

Dennis was right. There are some things that only God knows. In fact, there is absolutely nothing that God does *not* know. God knows the exact number of stars, planets, and asteroids in the universe. God knows the exact number of atoms that make up the paper and ink on this page. Jesus said that even the hairs of our heads are numbered (Luke 12:7). God knows the intimate details of each of our lives and what we are thinking right now.

"If God knows everything, and He knows what I'm going to say to Him before I say it, then why say it?"

Have you ever thought about that? Why pray? What's the point of telling God something He already knows? Why do I need to ask God for things He's already decided to give me? Or why take the time to ask God for things

He's already decided *not* to give me? If God loves me, isn't He going to do what is best for me anyway?

Interesting questions. But we still pray, don't we?

The Urge to Pray

Who are you? If I asked you to describe yourself in a letter, how would you do it? Would you describe the color of your eyes and hair, your height, weight and shoe size? You would probably describe yourself physically.

But there is more to us than just our physical bodies. We were also designed and created with a soul and a spirit. The soul is made up of the mind, will, and emotions. Our minds are the thinking part of who we are. Our emotions are the way we feel or the moods we get. Our will is the part of us that decides what we're going to do. We've all had those times when we struggled with a decision. You may have said, "My head is telling me one thing, but my heart is telling me another." That was your mind and emotions trying to tell you what to do, but it was your will that decided which one to listen to.

But it is our spirits that make us so very special. The Bible says that man was created in the image of God. We were made into spiritual beings just as God is a spiritual being. Our spirit is that part of us that was designed to know God and be friends with God.

There's a problem, though. Although we were created to walk with God and commune with God, our sin has broken that relationship. And because we can no longer interact with God as we were intended, our spirits are useless. As long as we are controlled by sin, our spirits are lifeless and empty.

Big Man on Campus

Sol was incredible. There was nothing he couldn't do . . . or hadn't tried. Sol had things of which other people only dream. He was so rich that there was nothing he couldn't buy. He was extremely smart. He was good-looking. And he was popular. What more could *anyone* ask for?

But Sol wanted more. He seemed to have everything *except* the one thing that would make him happy. What was it? He wasn't sure, but he was determined to find it.

Sol decided the answer was *more!* More of everything. Sol threw himself into his career and became even more successful. Another dollar, another house, another gadget, but never another step closer to finding his answer. His answer never came in his bank statement.

Perhaps, Sol thought, *I need to dig a little deeper for my answer. I'll go back to school and see what I can learn.* With each course completed, Sol added a few more hours to his college transcript, but he was still dissatisfied.

Sol changed his game plan. *I've got to quit trying so hard. Kick back, Sol, enjoy life. Lose yourself in a good time.* Sol became a party animal. And with all his money, it wasn't hard for him to buy friends and get whatever he needed to laugh, party, and enjoy himself. The thrills came and went, but the dissatisfaction never left. (See the book of Ecclesiates to read about Solomon and how he solved his dilemma.)

Square Pegs in Round Holes

All of us experience that incomplete feeling. Our bodies are alive, our souls are alive, but our spirits are dead and hollow. We instinctively try to fill that empty part within ourselves. Like Sol, we might try to satisfy that emptiness with money, possessions, pleasures, or philosophies. But since our spirits are shaped in the image of God's Spirit, the only thing that can fill that emptiness is God.

Too many people waste their time trying to fill that God-shaped emptiness with something other than God. This is why people worship. People worship the things they think will give their lives purpose and meaning. Some people worship the sun or the gods they believe live in trees or certain animals. Some people even worship other people. That's like trying to put square pegs in round holes. Only round pegs fit in round holes, and only God can fill the emptiness in us all.

People are religious because they were created to interact with God, and the most obvious way we can try to interact with God is through prayer. The problem is that most people don't know to *whom* they should pray.

So how can we know what this God is like? Enter Jesus Christ. Jesus Christ shows us who God is and how we can pray and interact with Him. He showed us who God is because He *is* God. As a carpenter from Nazareth, Jesus was God come to earth as a man.

By his death on the cross, Jesus removed the barrier of sin that had made our spirits dead. By His resurrection from the dead, He made our spirits alive so that we could have a personal relationship with God. This means that prayer is no longer a vain attempt to pray to *something*, but a personal interaction with the Creator of the universe through a relationship with Jesus Christ.

We still haven't answered the question, though, of *why* we should pray. We have only determined that it is *possible* for us to pray. To understand why we should pray, let's look at prayer from God's perspective.

Three Little Words

Maria was hurriedly putting on her makeup before making the mad rush to work. Ben was dressed and almost out the door when he stopped and turned around. He came back to where Maria was putting on her mascara and bent down to hug her. He held her silently for a few seconds and then whispered "I love you" in her ear. He kissed her lightly on the cheek before heading out the door.

Maria smiled to herself. They had only been married for six months, and it had been a wonderful six months. Ben was always surprising her with little ways of showing his love for her. He had always been like that. Right after they first met and began dating in school, he found ways to make her feel special. Phone calls. Cards. As their relationship deepened, so did Ben's expressions of love. Candle-lit dinners. Moonlit walks. Flowers for no special reason.

Maria smiled again. She knew that Ben loved her. There was no doubt in her mind, but she still liked to hear those three words, "I love you." Three simple spoken words. But that was the icing on the cake.

It's the same way with God. He knows our hearts. He knows if we love Him. He knows when we're sorry for our sinful actions. He knows what we want to ask Him. But He still wants to hear us say it. We should still pray because *God wants us to pray.* He loves and enjoys it when we pray. God loves our prayers because He loves us.

Wow! God, the great and awesome Creator of every atom and molecule in the universe, wants *my* company! God wants to be best friends with me!

God's Favorite Perfume

Gary had actually started to enjoy his geometry class. He struggled with the theorems, but he didn't mind the struggle so long as Trisha was sitting across from him. It was her perfume. Trisha never overdid it; she wore just enough of the enticing fragrance to catch his attention without overwhelming him. He was sure it had some wild, passionate or exotic name. Whatever it was called, this perfume attracted Gary to Trisha. Now if he could only work up the nerve to ask her out . . .

Perfume has one purpose: to please the senses and make us attractive to others. The Bible uses perfume to show how our prayers affect God. In the Old Testament the Israelites offered incense as a fragrant offering to God. Proverbs 27:9 says that "perfume and incense bring joy to the heart." The priests offered the incense to bring joy to the heart of God.

Wow! God, the great and awesome Creator of every molecule in the universe, wants my company!

When we pray, it is like perfume to God. Our prayers rise in the air, so to speak, as a fragrant offering to Him. God is pleased when we give our time and energy to talk to Him and come before His presence in prayer. That's why King David said in Psalm 141:2, "May my prayer be set before you like incense." David knew that his prayers brought joy to the heart of God just as perfume and incense did.

The apostle John saw firsthand how God delights in our prayers.

> Another angel, who had a golden censer, came and stood at the altar. He was given much incense to offer, with the prayers of all the saints, on the golden altar before the throne. The smoke of the incense, together with the prayers of the saints, went up before God from the angel's hand.
>
> Revelation 8:3–4

The divorce was final today. Julianne was told by an unknown judge in a cold courtroom that she would be living with her mother. Her mother was moving across the country to "start over," and Julianne cried into the pillow she was hugging. The thought of leaving her friends, her school, and her church was upsetting. The divorce and family problems were hard enough, and she knew it would be harder without the support of her friends at church.

Julianne didn't know what to do. All she could do was pray. "Dear God," she began, praying through her tears, "I don't want to go, but I must. Help me make this move. Help me find a good church and make new friends. I know you love me. I love you, too. Please help me."

On the other side of creation, there were thousands and thousands of voices singing the most incredible music. Unlike anything we have ever experienced here on earth, incredible uncountable voices were singing extraordinary melodies, accompanied by the sounds of all creation: the peals of thunder, the dance of lights, the roars of a million forces of nature. All in perfect harmony. The sole audience of this spectacular concert was God Himself.

A simple, soft-spoken prayer could hardly be heard in the midst of all this noise and music, but a pleasant fragrance rose through the multitudes and caught the attention of God. It was Julianne's prayer. And it captured God's heart.

A simple prayer. A fragrant perfume. A delight to God.

▼

Why does God enjoy our prayers so much? Our prayers are an expression of our love for Him and our need for Him. God never forces anyone to pray. We pray because it is our own choice to do so.

I have two sons who like to draw, and they are continually giving me their works of art. One day I came home from work to be greeted by my oldest son holding out a homemade envelope.

"It's for you, Dad," he exclaimed excitedly. I opened the envelope to find a piece of paper haphazardly folded up to fit inside the envelope. The piece of paper was a drawing in vivid crayon colors. "It's a giraffe, Dad!"

Although I am always glad to receive these works of art, do I *need* a picture of a giraffe? No. (In fact, I'm not sure it's a giraffe even after I have been told it's a giraffe.) I don't *need* the picture, but I *want* it because it's an expression of love from my preschool son. No one asked him to do it. He did it simply to please me.

God doesn't need our prayers. He created the entire universe without a single one of us praying. God can do anything and He doesn't need anything. But He still wants our prayers simply because He enjoys us, and the prayers please Him.

We Need It!

Why did Julianne cry and pray to God? She was hurting, afraid, and feeling alone. She needed God—just like we all do. While God may take great delight in our fellowship with Him through prayer, we desperately need fellowship with Him as well.

Our tendency is to pray when we are in trouble and have our backs against the wall. But it is not always like that. Some days can be a bed of roses and we may subconsciously think, *I don't need to pray today.* But Jesus said, "Apart from me you can do nothing" (John 15:5). If we think through even the most routine days of our lives, we will find that there is still a need for God's help in our lives.

Think about your relationship with your parents. Is it hard not to talk back and argue with them sometimes? Then you need to pray.

I'm sure there are students at school with whom it's hard to get along. What about the teacher who may treat you unfairly? Perhaps there is a class in which you are struggling (either you can't keep up or you can't keep awake). If any of these sound familiar, you need to pray.

Many times our human nature cries out, "I don't need help!" But if we're honest, we do need help. And when we admit our need for God's help through prayer, that's when things really begin to happen!

Why Doesn't God Just Make It Happen?

"Why doesn't God instantly make my life better? God knows what's best for me and I am willing to let Him do whatever He wants to make my life ideal. If God would automatically do that, life would be easier."

God could do that, but many times He waits. He waits for us to pray before He works. He wants us to have the opportunity to take part in His great work.

God wants us to experience the joy and thrill of being a part of His work. He not only wants us as His children, but also as His coworkers (1 Thessalonians 3:2). It's a great feeling to be part of God's family and even more incredible to know God trusts you and me to work with Him for His kingdom.

I think about the times I've had the privilege of leading someone to Christ. What excitement! God gets the glory, that person gets a new life, and I get an overwhelming sense of joy. God used me! I played a part in the kingdom of God that will last for eternity!

You and I can experience that same joy when we pray. As we lift our needs or concerns to God, He takes those prayers and unleashes His power. Lives are changed. Answers are found. Problems disappear. God is glorified because He's the one who answered the need, but we still get that overwhelming sense of joy because God allowed us to see His hand at work. Prayer unleashes the power of God and that's exciting!

▼

The President Is on the Line

Jeff was glad to be home. His books made it no further than the bookshelf by the front door. The TV was on in a flash and Jeff immediately began flipping through the channels with the remote control as he headed for the kitchen. He was quickly back with a bag of chips, a bowl of picante sauce, and a Coke. He plopped down on the couch and never gave a thought to the homework waiting for him. The only thought he had was, "With sixty channels, there's bound to be something to watch."

The Skipper was about to hit Gilligan with his hat when the telephone rang. *Mom making sure I got home,* Jeff thought. He picked up the phone. "Hello."

The voice on the other end was businesslike. Even polite. Certainly none of Jeff's friends. "Hello, may I speak with Jeff Crayson?"

"Yeah . . . I mean, yes, ma'am . . . uh, this is Jeff."

"I am Joan Smith, the personal secretary to the president. He would like to speak with you."

"The president? Of what?" he asked, not thinking.

"The United States." There was silence while the secretary waited for a response. She said again, "The president would like to speak to you."

Jeff quickly swallowed the chip in his mouth and ran a hand through his hair as though the secretary was standing in front of him. He blurted, "Uh, sure. Yeah . . . er, yes, ma'am."

There was silence on the line for a minute and then Jeff heard a very familiar voice. "Hello, Jeff, this is . . ."

"Yes, sir, I know who you are!" Jeff exclaimed before he realized what he was saying.

The president asked Jeff about his school and classwork, and about his family. He asked a lot of general questions and seemed genuinely interested in Jeff. All the time, Jeff was wondering, *Why is he asking me this?*

Finally the president said, "Jeff, there is a reason I wanted to talk to you. Are you familiar with the Education Reform Bill?"

"A little. Not very much," Jeff replied. Jeff felt like he had disappointed the president and expected him to end the conversation and hang up.

"This is a very important matter, Jeff, and there are several sides to the issue. This will greatly affect students and I wanted to get a student's opinion. May I explain the issue to you?"

For the next fifteen minutes, the president explained the Education Reform Bill to Jeff. Jeff listened intently, as he had never listened before. At the close of his explanation, the president asked, "Now, Jeff, if you were in my shoes, what would you do?"

"Well . . . ?" Jeff hesitated.

"I want your honest reaction, Jeff," the president interrupted, "What would you do?"

With more "sirs" than he had ever used in his lifetime, Jeff explained what he thought was the best approach and why. The president listened quietly and then thanked him.

"Jeff, you have been most helpful. I will consider what you just said as I decide what to do. Thanks. Your parents should be proud." With that, the president hung up.

Two days later, Jeff ran in from school. The books stayed in his hands, his shoes stayed on his feet, but he did go for the remote control. No Gilligan today, though. Jeff went straight to the cable news network. Since his private conversation with the president, Jeff's interest in current affairs had changed drastically, and he was constantly checking the news for reports about the Education Reform Bill.

Jeff was not disappointed today. His TV had been on only a few minutes when the newscaster said, "Today, the

president signed the historic Education Reform Bill . . ."
Jeff inched to the edge of the chair. He listened as the
newscaster explained the bill and showed video footage
of the president signing the bill.

The news then had a clip of the president speaking.

"The importance of this bill came to me through the
eyes of a high school student. I made a friend this week
who helped me see the impact of this bill on his own life
as a student."

Jeff jumped off the chair and shouted. He picked up
the phone and began to call each one of his friends and
tell them, "Hey! The president followed my advice!" Jeff
realized, though, that no one knew this except the president and him. Who would believe him if he told them?
He put the phone down and went to the kitchen for the
bag of chips. The president may have gotten all the credit
for this major decision, but Jeff felt an unshakable ex-
hilaration knowing he had a hand in the president's
work.

▼

We have a privilege every day to talk to somebody far
more important and far more powerful than the president of the United States: God Himself. This almighty,
holy, awesome Creator wants us to have the privilege of
participating in His work. As God works, He gets all the
glory, but we get an incredible sense of joy knowing we
were a part of His work. What an opportunity! And all
we have to do is talk to Him.

Why pray? God wants it, we need it, and it makes
incredible things happen.

▼

A C T S
– Responding to What I Read –

Adoration. Praise God for His incredible love. In spite of our sinfulness, He loved us enough to die for us so that we could have an intimate relationship with Him and be able to pray to Him.

Confession. Admit to God if you have not bothered to pray or have taken the privilege of prayer for granted. Confess to God if you have tried to do things on your own without relying on His help.

Thanksgiving. Thank God for the opportunity to be involved in His work through prayer. Thank Him for the privilege of communing with Him and being His co-worker.

Supplication. Ask God to help you be a better pray-er. Ask Him to take the control of your life and meet your needs through His power. Ask Him to show you different ways you can pray for others and help with His kingdom's work.

▼

T W O

Learning from the Master

One of his disciples said to him,
"Lord, teach us to pray."
Luke 11:1

▼

The assignment was for each student give an oral report on one person who had made a significant impact on the world. For Mr. Parrish, it promised to be a parade of the usual names, numbers, and accomplishments delivered in the usual monotone reading voice. He heard the expected reports on Washington, Lincoln, and Edison. A few of the more astute students gave reports on Charlemagne, Napoleon, and Socrates. The most entertaining was from Jenny Benson who reported on Alexander Graham Bell and his telephone, which had personally revolutionized her social life.

Then it was Holly's turn. She was one of Mr. Parrish's quieter students, but she successfully masked her nervousness behind a face of determination. She silently eyed her classmates before she spoke.

"Before I give my report on a significant person , I want to read something I found hanging on a wall at my grandmother's." Holly paused and pulled a crumpled piece of paper out from behind her report. This is what she read:

He was born in an obscure village, the child of a peasant woman. He worked in a carpenter shop until He was thirty. He then became an itinerant preacher. He never held an office. He never had a family nor owned a house. He didn't go to college. He never wrote a book. He never did any of the things that usually accompany greatness. He had no credentials but Himself. He was only thirty-three when the public turned against Him. His friends ran away. He was turned over to His enemies, went through the mockery of a trial, and sentenced to death. While He was dying, His executioners gambled for His clothing, the only property He had on earth. He was laid in a borrowed grave.

Nineteen centuries have come and gone, and today He is the central figure of the human race. All the armies that ever marched, all the navies that ever sailed, all the parliaments that ever sat, and all the kings that ever reigned, have not affected the life of man on this earth as much as this one life.

Holly looked up and saw that every eye was fixed on her. She swallowed hard and said, "My report is on Jesus Christ, *the* most significant Person in history."

▼

There has never been another person on earth like Jesus. In so many ways, His life was simple, yet look at what He accomplished! Jesus gave the crowds teachings that challenged their religious habits and showed them the way to live an abundant life. Jesus met people's needs for food or health. He gave back to individuals their sight, their limbs, their minds, and their lives. Jesus opened people's spiritual eyes to see how they could have a real and personal relationship with God. And Jesus did this all in three brief years! He changed the course of history.

Now comes the incredible part. Jesus said, "I tell you the truth, anyone who has faith in me will do what I have been doing. He will do even greater things than these, because I am going to the Father" (John 14:12). Can you imagine doing greater things than Jesus did?

What would it take for us to do greater things? This verse says it takes faith in Him. We must trust Jesus and live in dependence on Him just as He trusted His Father and lived in dependence on Him.

Jesus expressed His faith, trust and dependence on the Father through His life of prayer. Jesus spent a lot of time in prayer. It seems that if anybody *didn't* need to pray, it would be the Son of God. But just the opposite is true: Jesus relied heavily on prayer. If Jesus needed to pray, then you and I certainly need to pray. To see why *we* ought to pray, let's look at why Jesus prayed.

> If Jesus needed to pray, then you and I certainly need to pray.

Jesus Prayed for Communion

Imagine what heaven must be like. Picture in your mind the absolute best of everything.

No matter what we picture in our minds, God's heaven goes far beyond anything we can imagine. In the middle of all this beauty and majesty sits God on His throne. He created everything and all creation sings of the greatness of God. But God the Son voluntarily stepped down from His spectacular throne and came to earth as a little baby.

Being a human is quite different from sitting in the center of heaven and all creation and being worshiped. One moment the throne of heaven, the next moment a musty cradle among barnyard animals. One moment the songs of heaven, the next moment His own infant cries from hunger.

Have you ever wondered what it would be like to be an amoeba? Probably not. What's there to wonder about? Who would want to be a one-celled organism that does . . . well, nothing? If we were amoebas, we'd miss all the thrill of life. No friends nor family. No music. No excitement from sports. No pizza. Nothing. Who in their right mind would give up all the experiences of being a human being to become an amoeba? But that's the kind of drastic change Jesus made when He gave up all the joy and majesty of heaven to become a human! By comparison to what He had, Jesus made Himself *nothing*.

What does this have to do with prayer? Jesus remembered the wonderful times of communion and fellowship with God the Father and God the Holy Spirit while seated on His throne in heaven. As a human, Jesus was not able to experience the same degree of intimacy with His Father. That's why Jesus prayed. He relished those times of being with His Father.

It is unfortunate that the average dictionary defines prayer as *asking*. That's usually how we use prayer, too. We pray only when we want to make a request of God. Many times, though, Jesus prayed simply in order to *be* with His father.

When I moved to Tennessee, I had to leave my family temporarily in Texas. It was difficult being away from my wife and sons for those six weeks. But every evening, without fail, we would talk on the telephone. Fifteen, twenty, thirty minutes each evening on the phone. Our phone bill got expensive, but it was worth it. Why? Just because we missed each other. There were occasions when we discussed business matters, but usually we called just to hear each other's voice. Just to say hello.

While Jesus walked this earth, He missed the communion He had with His Father in heaven. But prayer was the next best thing to being there. That's why Jesus often went up into the mountains alone. He just wanted to commune with His Father.

▼

The Saturday morning cartoons were over so Nathan decided to cruise around the neighborhood on his bike. He stepped into the garage to get his bicycle and discovered a huge mess with his dad at the center of it all.

"What's all this, Dad?" asked Nathan.

"It's a cabinet and bookcase for your sister's room," replied his father.

A cabinet and a bookcase. All Nathan saw was a small stack of lumber, some plywood, an assortment of nails and screws on the concrete floor, and a collection of power tools with their cords tangled together.

"Looks more like a mess to me," said Nathan.

"Stick around. There's a cabinet and bookcase here," replied his father.

Nathan smiled as he thought back to that moment almost ten years earlier. He remembered spending the rest of that Saturday watching his dad transform a pile of wood into a cabinet.

And now Nathan was standing in shop class putting the finishing touches on his own cabinet—a cabinet he had made himself. He stood back and admired his work. It looked great. Nathan realized that he was able to do this only because he had spent many Saturdays in the garage learning, listening, and being guided by his father in the art of woodwork.

Jesus Prayed for Guidance

Jesus, too, listened to His Father for guidance and direction. Jesus' earthly ministry was short—three quick years—yet the decisions He made during that time were lasting. Jesus prayed for guidance to make sure He made the right decisions.

Jesus knew His time on earth was short. He was going to have to leave His work for others to carry on. Jesus chose twelve men to train and teach, so that when He had returned to His throne in heaven, these men would be equipped and capable of carrying on His ministry. But Jesus didn't choose the twelve men hastily.

Jesus went out to a mountainside to pray, and spent the night praying to God. When morning came, he called his disciples to him and chose twelve of them, whom he also designated apostles.

Luke 6:12–13

If the twelve disciples had to be chosen today, whom would *you* choose to carry on this great work? The president of the student body? The star athlete? A rich and successful business person? What about a rock star or celebrity? These people are popular, they have power and influence, or they're well-known. Who better to spread the good news of Christ quickly?

But God approaches His work differently. "The Lord does not look at the things man looks at. Man looks at the outward appearance, but the Lord looks at the heart" (1 Samuel 16:7). He knew the hearts of these twelve men. He knew inside a fisherman named Peter were the makings of a great church leader. He knew a despised tax collector named Matthew would become most effective in spreading the good news.

Jesus said on one occasion, "I have come down from heaven not to do my will but to do the will of him who sent me" (John 6:38). By praying, Jesus made sure that He was always staying in touch with the program and purpose of His Father.

By praying, Jesus made sure that He was always staying in touch with the program and purpose of His Father.

▼

Sharon climbed into bed, glad the day was over. Most sixteen-year-old girls would rather stay up talking with friends on the telephone, but Sharon decided the sooner she went to sleep, the sooner this day would be over.

It had not been a good day. She got up late because she had stayed up late the night before trying to finish the closing chapters of *The Scarlet Letter* working on her essay about the book. She rushed through breakfast, getting as much strawberry jam on her jacket as she did on her toast. Because she took time to try, unsuccessfully, to clean the stain off the jacket, Sharon missed the school bus. Her mother was not happy about having to drive Sharon to the high school, since it would make her late for work, and she dutifully nagged Sharon all during the car ride. "You're late, so I'm late . . . You left your room in a mess . . . You left strawberry jam all over the kitchen counter . . . You need to be more responsible . . . You make me look irresponsible."

School was no better. The custodians had waxed the hall floors the night before, and, hurrying to beat the bell, Sharon slipped on the slick floor, spilling her books and essay and embarrassing herself in front of three members of the varsity basketball team. She could still hear the remark, "What a graceful athlete," as she slipped into her chair ten seconds after the final bell echoed. This was Sharon's fourth tardy. Detention hall.

The day never got any better. She did get her English essay turned in, but it was covered with strawberry jam. The crowning blow came that afternoon. The volleyball teams were posted. Sharon didn't make the cut.

Sharon lay in bed, in the darkness, feeling like the whole world was against her. *I hope tomorrow is less of a challenge.*

Jesus Prayed for Strength

Jesus found this earthly life to be a challenge, too. Day after day, Jesus was bombarded by people wanting to be healed or fed, wanting to see another miracle, and wanting to challenge His teaching and authority. Demands, demands, demands. Can you imagine how physically and emotionally draining that must have been? That's another reason Jesus prayed. He prayed for strength. He stayed in touch with His Father, the source of His power. It's difficult to imagine Jesus needing strength after all the incredible miracles He performed, but He did.

The hardest time for Jesus was His last night on earth. He knew He was about to be arrested, tried, crucified, and abandoned by His friends. It was going to be, literally, Him against the world. Jesus faced a degree of discouragement and fatigue that we can't even imagine. But Jesus went to His Father for strength.

The physical pain that Jesus endured on the cross was incredible, but equally incredible was the mental anguish that Jesus endured in the garden of Gethsemane. He sweated drops of blood. While in such great anguish, Jesus prayed for strength to carry on. The heart of His hours of prayer that night was, "My Father, if it is possible, may this cup be taken from me. Yet not as I will, but as you will" (Matthew 26:39).

Make no mistake: Jesus would have walked away from all this if He could. But He knew that giving in to the human part of Himself that said "Don't do it!" would not accomplish what He came to earth to do: free us from our sins. So Jesus prayed for strength.

Did His Father strengthen Him? He sure did! When the crowds arrived to arrest Him, they did not see a weak man who cowered. Jesus set His will to do His Father's will, and because of the strength God gave Him, He was determined to go through with it. The prophet Isaiah foretold these words of Jesus:

> Because the Sovereign LORD helps me, I will not be
> disgraced. Therefore have I set my face like flint, and
> I know I will not be put to shame.
>
> Isaiah 50:7

Jesus prayed for strength . . . and got it. The Father strengthened Jesus—so much so that He set His composure like a rock and walked into the trials, crucifixion, and death without flinching.

Those times that Jesus prayed for fellowship or guidance or strength were not just sporadic occasional prayers. For most of us, though, prayer is simply another part of our lives; for Jesus, prayer was His life. Jesus maintained a constant attitude of prayer. His frame of mind was to be always in touch with His Father.

Jesus prayed often. He often withdrew to lonely places and prayed (Luke 5:16). Statements such as this are found over and over again in the gospel accounts of the life of Jesus. Jesus didn't just pray on an occasional basis, such as right before a big sermon or miracle. Jesus was *constantly* praying. He was habitually getting alone with His Father for communion, guidance, and strength.

If Jesus Needed to Pray, Then So Do I!

I'm a lot further from an intimate relationship with God than Jesus; so if Jesus made communion with God a priority, then I certainly need to make it a priority. If Jesus found it necessary to pray for strength and guidance, then I certainly should, too.

Jesus said, "I tell you the truth, anyone who has faith in me will do what I have been doing. He will do even greater things than these, because I am going to the Father" (John 14:12). How can you and I accomplish even greater things than Jesus? By having a prayer life like Jesus. Yes, if we gave prayer the place in our lives that Jesus gave it in His life, we, too, could accomplish the most incredible things for God!

Is it possible? You say that you've never seen nor heard of it being done? Maybe so. It's been said, "No man ever accomplished more than Jesus because no man ever devoted as much time to prayer." Will you be the one to challenge that statement? Will you be the one to accomplish great things just like Jesus . . . and even more?

It's possible.

It begins with prayer.

▼

A   C   T   S
—Responding to What I Read—

Adoration. Praise God for making you a person of worth and value. You are a person of value because the Father cares as much about you as He does about His Son, Jesus Christ. Your prayers are just as important as Jesus' prayers. Praise God for always being there to hear you pray as He was always available to hear His Son pray.

Confession. If you have taken for granted the need for prayer or have dismissed the importance of talking to God, admit that to God. Tell God that you want to take your prayer life more seriously—just like Jesus did.

Thanksgiving. Hebrews 4:15 tells us that Jesus is not "a high priest who is unable to sympathize with our weaknesses, but we have one who has been tempted in every way, just as we are—yet was without sin." Thank God for identifying with us in our humanness. Thank Him for His example in life and in prayer.

Supplication. Ask God to teach you to pray like Jesus prayed. Ask Him to help you understand the principles in the Model Prayer that you are about to learn, so that you can pray effectively.

▼

T H R E E

Who Ya Gonna Call?

Our Father in heaven.
Matthew 6:9

▼

Keith maneuvered through the cafeteria tables to find his usual lunch crowd in an animated discussion. He put his tray of veggies and mystery meat down next to Bruce. Before he sat down he realized this wasn't the usual cafeteria conversation.

"So there we sit, not knowing what to do," said Kevin, gesturing with a ketchup-logged French fry. "One girl actually bows her head, but the rest of us just sort of . . . stare. 'Cept for Lon here. He's busy admiring his muscles." He nudged Lon and everybody laughed.

Lon attempted to direct the conversation away from himself. "Yeah, well, what's the point of a minute of silence? Who's going to pray? I mean, what's the point of praying? God doesn't care about your little dweeb life. He's just on a cloud somewhere plucking a harp."

Bruce shook his head. "No, you got God figured all wrong. God'll do stuff for you if you ask Him. You just got to play by His rules. I pray." He paused when he saw the looks he got from Lon and Kevin. "Yeah, that's right.

I figure it doesn't hurt to ask. On those days when I've been more good than bad, God gives me what I ask."

"So what do you ask?" asked Bruce.

Bruce paused. "Stuff," he said, quickly filling his mouth with soybean hamburger.

Kevin picked up another soggy French fry and said, "You've got folks saying 'Hail Marys.' Like my mom. Others are sitting out there in wacko positions saying one word over and over again. Others talk in weird languages. Sit on a flagpole. Hang out in monasteries. And they're all trying to get in touch with God."

"And we're supposed to get in touch with God during the first period minute of silence," said Lon.

"What about you, Keith?" asked Lon. "Do you pray?"

Keith summed it up for the group. "Maybe I'd talk to God if I knew who I was talking to."

▼

What kind of God are we trying to talk to? What is He like? How should we approach the Creator of the universe? To get a good handle on what we should pray *for*, we need to get a good handle on whom we pray *to*.

We all have special friends we know really well. And they know us equally well. We share special words or inside jokes that don't mean anything to anybody else except us. We see our friends in the hall, slap them on the back, call them by some silly nickname, and immediately pick up the conversation where we left it an hour ago.

Would we do the same thing with the school principal? Imagine walking up to the principal, slapping him on the back, playfully messing up his hair and saying, "Hey, old timer, seen any good movies lately?" And imagine the principal's response!

What makes the difference? Our relationship with a best friend is different from our relationship with the school principal. How we talk with others depends on what kind of relationship we have with them.

What does this have to do with prayer? The kind of relationship we think we have with God will affect how we pray. Is He like that best friend, or is He more like a feared school principal? When you think of God, what kind of personality do you imagine? Let's look first at some misunderstandings people often have about the personality of God.

Who God Is . . . Not!

The Policeman God

Some people think of God as a policeman. He is constantly looking over our shoulders, ready and waiting to pounce on us when we step out of line. The policeman God is on the constant lookout for sin in our lives, and when we sin . . . wham! He lets us know it. He convicts us of sin by making us feel really miserable. We get sick. Our grades drop at school. We get dropped by a boyfriend or girlfriend. The policeman God will inflict punishment on us because we have sinned and deserve to be punished.

But the policeman God also rewards good behavior. Just as the law-abiding citizen need not fear the local policeman, the law-abiding Christian need not fear the policeman God. God rewards those who are faithful and obedient. If we have not sinned or stepped out of line, then God will answer our prayers.

When people pray to the policeman God, they may spend a lot of time dwelling on their sin. They spend a lot of time begging and pleading for God to forgive them. Or they try to bargain with God, just like a person may try to talk a policeman out of giving him a ticket.

"Help me pass this test and I'll . . . ."

"God, get me into this college and I'll . . . ."

"Do this for me and I'll do this for you."

The truth, though, is that we don't have to bargain with God. God is not like a policeman. Yes, He is concerned about the sin in our lives. And, yes, God will discipline us many times to bring us back into right relationship with Him. But God's concern and discipline are deeply rooted in one other aspect of His character: love. God's desire is not to punish but to forgive.

The Lord is not slow in keeping his promise, as some understand slowness. He is patient with you, not wanting anyone to perish, but everyone to come to repentance.

2 Peter 3:9

If God loves us, why does He discipline us? His discipline is intended to lead us away from the harmful path we are on back into His care and guidance. God's discipline is firm, but it is guided by love.

It is reassuring to know that we don't have to "cut a deal" with God. Instead, we just need to confess our sins and get on with living the life God wants us to enjoy.

The Grandfatherly God

Some people's idea of God is just the opposite of the policeman God. Their God is like a kind, old grandfather. He's a nice old man to have around, even though He's not always in tune with the real world. He smiles a lot, loves a lot, and tends to overlook the wrong in our lives.

This is the kind of grandfather that is great to have around as a kid. If Dad couldn't take us to the game nor to the store, just ask Granddad. He'd take us. If we got in trouble with Dad, Granddad would speak in our defense and try to get Dad to ease up on the punishment.

Jesus Christ is always there to speak in our defense, but that doesn't mean He will let us get away with anything we please. He wants the best for us, but His holiness and His desire for our best will not let Him dismiss our sins.

Just like a grandfather, He wants the best for us, but we have to trust Him to show us what is best.

The Santa Claus God

Other people carry the image of a grandfatherly God a step further. They see Him more like Santa Claus. He's not only this kind, jolly old person who loves us, but He'll give us *whatever* we ask for.

"God created everything, *right?* There's nothing God cannot do, *right?* So it's really no big deal for God to be able to give me this one thing, *right?*" Many people outgrow their belief in Santa Claus, but they believe in a God that is supposed to make them happy by giving them everything they want.

▼

Keith pushed the rewind button on the VCR. He and his best friend, Chris, had just finished watching the latest Clyde Van Dorn movie. It was a typical Van Dorn movie, one in which he single-handedly fights at least one thousand ruthless bad guys and saves the civilized world from destruction. Keith and Chris were pumped; they talked about how cool it would be to act like Van Dorn.

At that moment, Keith's dad walked through the den where Keith and Chris were planning to save the world. "Hey, Dad," asked Keith excitedly, "Do you have a gun I could borrow?"

"I don't own a gun," muttered his dad without much thought.

"Well, could we go buy a gun?"

That caught his father's attention. "A gun? What in the world do we need to buy a gun for?"

"Aw, we're just wanting to act out a movie. Chase out the bad guys and stuff. You know, holding a *real* gun would make it more realistic."

"A gun?! To play with?!" interrupted his father. "You don't *play* with guns."

Keith reacted angrily, without thinking. "Aw, gee, Dad, c'mon. You never give me anything I ask for!"

Dad surveyed the den. Video games were stacked against the wall waiting to be played. Keith's expensive basketball shoes lay in the corner. The remains of a large pepperoni pizza lay in a pizza box. *No,* he told himself, *I do provide for my son. And good things, too. But that doesn't include a gun. He is too young to handle something so deadly and dangerous.* The only thing Keith's father questioned was the wisdom of letting his ten-year-old son watch Clyde Van Dorn movies.

Parents give things to their children because they love them. But parents may also withhold things from their children for the same reason. Keith's father was keeping his son's best interests at heart. Would giving Keith a gun to play with be loving? No. It may have been what Keith wanted, but it wasn't what was best for Keith.

It's the same with God. God is not some sort of heavenly vending machine, giving us whatever we ask for. Put a quarter in, make your request of God, and out it comes! No, it doesn't work that way. God does want to do things for us, but His giving is always coated with love. God gives what is good and always gives what is best.

The Force

The *Star Wars* series gave us that memorable line, "May the force be with you." The force is an incredible power that we, like Luke Skywalker, can harness. There's something magical and mystical about this power, and if we know how to tap into it, we can accomplish great things. The secret is learning how to tap into this great power.

People get involved in the New Age movement to try to tap into this power. Hinduism claims that this force is within each of us and we must find it within ourselves. New religions are constantly popping up claiming to have the secret to God and to this force.

> God's working in our lives is not based on rules, but on a relationship.

Even Christians often treat God like a force. "Read the Bible and learn how to get this power into your life." "There is a certain way to pray that will unleash God's power." "Follow this routine or ritual and see what happens." Christianity is reduced to mystical and magical formulas.

God is not a force that can be automatically used at our bidding by following certain laws, rituals or rules.

God is a Person. God's working in our lives is not based on rules, but on a relationship.

The Right Picture of God

If God is a person, what is He like? What kind of relationship can I have with God? Jesus gives us the answer in four words. Those words begin the Model Prayer: Our Father in heaven.

God is our Father.

Try to imagine the perfect father. Take away all the negative images and think of only the positive qualities you think a father ought to have. What would he be like? Here are six characteristics of the perfect Father.

He Loves Unconditionally

The perfect Father does not say, "I love you because you go to church."

"I love you because you work hard at school."

"I love you because you don't lie or cheat or steal."

No conditions. The perfect Father just loves us. In fact, He loves us in spite of ourselves. If this Father said, "I love you because . . ." then He could also say, "I no longer love you because of the way you treated your mother yesterday." Instead, He just says, "I love you." No becauses.

There is nothing we can do to make this Father love us any more. Nor is there anything we can do to make Him love us any less. He loves us. Unconditionally. Yes, there are times that we disappoint God our Father. But He still loves us.

God's unconditional love doesn't mean we can sin all we want. God takes our sin seriously and may discipline us to pull us away from harmful sin and back into a right relationship with Him.

Love and discipline? Does that sound contradictory? Think of God as a loving coach. A good coach wants you to win. He's going to do everything he can to see that you win. That means he is going to discipline you. He's going to push you to run. Run. Run. Run some more. Run until you don't think you can go another step. No high-calorie desserts. Plenty of rest. And (sigh) more running.

Is the coach mean? No, he's only trying to bring out your best. God's discipline is the same. God loves you and wants you to reach your full potential in Him, but it may take discipline.

Endure hardship as discipline; God is treating you as sons. For what son is not disciplined by his father? . . . Our fathers disciplined us for a little while as they thought best; but God disciplines us for our good, that we may share in his holiness. No discipline seems pleasant at the time, but painful. Later on, however, it produces a harvest of righteousness and peace for those who have been trained by it.

Hebrews 12:7, 10–11

If God didn't love us, then He wouldn't care what we did. But He does love us and wants the very best for us. God's incredible love for us should motivate us to love Him in return and live a life that pleases him. "We love because he first loved us" (1 John 4:19).

He Protects

When I was a young boy, my family went camping in the Ozarks of Arkansas. The scenery was great. The countless trees and hills were exciting to a young boy used to the flat landscape of the Texas Gulf Coast.

Near our campsite was a large hill just waiting to be climbed. I couldn't resist such an adventure. The problem was that the hill was extremely steep. I gave no thought to this, though, as I held on to rocks and roots, inching my way to the top.

When I had climbed as high as I could go, I turned and looked down on our campsite. I suddenly realized how high I had climbed and how difficult it would be to get back down. I called out to my dad, saying, "Hey, look at me!" It was a call of excitement, not fear. But my father saw the bigger picture; he saw the dangerous spot I was in. So my dad's response was to climb up the side of that hill to where I was and help me down. No scolding, just his guidance and protection in getting me out of a difficult situation.

The perfect Father is constantly watching out for His children. He doesn't want any harm to come to them.

He will cover you with his feathers, and under his wings you will find refuge; his faithfulness will be your shield and rampart. You will not fear the terror of night, nor the arrow that flies by day, nor the pestilence that stalks in the darkness, nor the plague that destroys at midday. A thousand may fall at your side, ten thousand at your right hand, but it will not come near you.

Psalm 91:4–7

God our Father is able to protect us because He is omnipotent. That means He is all powerful. God has the power and ability to do anything He wants. "With God all things are possible" (Matthew 19:26). God is on my side! There is nothing from which He cannot free me nor protect me. He is my Father, I am His child, and He will see that His child is safe.

He Takes Away Fear

When you were a small child, did you ever have a monster under your bed? Lots of kids do. They are convinced that some mutated green and orange slime creature is lurking under their bed waiting to devour them as soon as they fall asleep. So they call for help. Dad comes in, turns on the light and either convinces them that there is no monster there or he "scares" the monster away. Either way, their fears are gone because Dad took care of the situation.

Sometimes the "monsters" we face are real. Sometimes they are only our own worries.

"I don't understand this class, and I'm going to fail!"

"How can I face her after what happened?"

"I don't want to move to another town. What if I don't like it there?"

"What's going to happen now that Mom is gone?"

The perfect Father doesn't want us to worry; He wants us to trust His love and protection. We may not see how it's all going to end up, but we can trust that God will love us and protect us through whatever we are facing.

The Lord is with me; I will not be afraid. What can man do to me? The Lord is with me; he is my helper.
Psalm 118:6–7

He Cares

The perfect Father's love is evident in that He is interested in the things in our lives. He's not like Vanessa's aunt. Vanessa's aunt is a relative that Vanessa sees only once a year at the family reunion. Aunt Martha waddles over to Vanessa and goes on and on about how Vanessa has grown. "Why, I remember when you were in diapers and cried all the time! I love you, dearie."

As Aunt Martha turns to speak to another relative, Vanessa wonders if her aunt really does love her. *Aunt Martha doesn't know what is going on in my life,* she thinks, *and she never asks.*

> He cares about all aspects of our lives. There is nothing too "silly" or insignificant about which we cannot pray and talk to God.

The perfect Father, though, is interested and does care. He is not just interested in the big events in our lives—passing grades, choosing a college, choosing a career, finding someone to marry. He is equally interested in our day-to-day routine.

That's the kind of relationship our heavenly Father wants to have with each one of us. He cares about all aspects of our lives. There is nothing too "silly" or insignificant about which we cannot pray and talk to God. That's why Peter said to "cast all your anxiety on him because he cares for you" (1 Peter 5:7).

▼

Maria needed help. It was getting late and she was getting nowhere with her calculus assignment. "It just doesn't make sense," she concluded. Maria needed her dad. He was an engineer and understood this stuff. He could explain question three. But, unfortunately, he was away on business and would not return until Friday. And her assignment was due tomorrow. Maria slammed the book closed in resignation. If only her dad were here . . . .

He Is Always There

One of the best things about the perfect Father is that He is always there for His children. It doesn't matter when or where; your heavenly Father is there for you.

> Where can I go from your Spirit?
> Where can I flee from your presence?
> If I go up to the heavens, you are there;
> if I make my bed in the depths, you are there.
> If I rise on the wings of the dawn,
> if I settle on the far side of the sea,
> even there your hand will guide me,
> your right hand will hold me fast.
>
> Psalm 139:7–10

One of the great mysteries of God is that He is omnipresent. That means He is everywhere at the same time. He is with you right now as you are reading this book, He is across town with your best friend, and He is on the other side of the world loving someone. It's a mystery how He can be everywhere and hear everyone's prayers at the same time. Don't try to figure it out, just accept it. And remember: don't ever think that God is too busy to spend time with you. You are His child, and He is always there, always ready to hear you.

What an incredible Father! And that's who Jesus says we are praying to. A God who loves, protects, cares, and desires to work in our lives. A God who gives hope and takes away fear and loneliness. But the best part is that we are not limited just *to knowing* about such a heavenly Father; we can have a relationship with Him, too.

Abba Father

Another word for father used in the Bible is *Abba*. Abba is a more intimate word, like *daddy* or *papa*—a word babies would use when they called out, like a baby today might say, "Da-da." At the time the New Testament was written, slaves were not allowed to address their master as Abba. They could call him Father, showing that he was the head of the house, but never Abba. Only the true sons and daughters could intimately call their father Abba.

When we give our lives to Christ, we enter into a new relationship with God. No longer slaves to sin, we are forgiven and adopted into the family of God. Now, we can do more than just know about God, we can be personal and intimate with Him. "Because you are sons, God sent the Spirit of his Son into our hearts, the Spirit who calls out, 'Abba, Father' (Galatians 4:6).

Jesus began the Model Prayer with "Our Father in heaven." Jesus wants us to remember that this intimate, loving, caring Father is in heaven. He is abiding in our hearts and lives, but He is also in the heavens, over and above everything. Our prayer requests are brought to a loving, caring, intimate God, but they are also brought to a God who is able to do anything because He is the God over the heavens and everything in them.

Yes, He is an incredible Father! The entire universe is at His disposal. Every molecule and every atom are here because He spoke them into existence. Yes, this great God of the heavens is also our Father. In all His majesty and glory, in all His time of watching over stars and galaxies, He always has time to be our Friend and Father in prayer.

▼

A C T S
– Responding to What I Read –

Adoration. Praise God for all that He is. Praise Him for His heavenly majesty and power, and praise Him for His fatherly qualities. Think of the characteristics of a perfect father and praise God for having those same characteristics: understanding, love, sympathy, patience, goodness, etc.

Confession. Have you ever thought of God as a sort of policeman? Have you ever thought of God as just a kind, old grandfather or as Santa Claus, ready to give you whatever you want? Have you ever thought of God as some impersonal force, a power that you can use to your advantage? If so, admit it to God. Ask Him to keep you from having the wrong ideas about who He is as you pray.

Thanksgiving. Thank God for being the perfect Father. Think of some specific ways God has shown you His love or care. Thank Him for those specific ways He has expressed His love and care to you. Think of specific ways He has protected or guided you, and thank Him for those times of protection and guidance.

Supplication. Ask God for wisdom in seeing Him as He truly is. Ask Him to help you be the kind of child that doesn't just ask things, but prays out of love and a desire for fellowship.

▼

Getting Things Started

▼

Now that we have a better understanding of God as a powerful and loving Father, we can think about the types of things we can ask of such a perfect Father. The Model Prayer that Jesus gave us in Matthew 6:9–13 can be divided into six requests or things we ask of God.

These six requests are not to be prayed word for word, but they represent *types* of things we ask of God. You might be amazed to find that everything you can pray to God about can be found in one of these six requests.

We'll begin with the first three requests—requests that don't center around us, but center around God! Jesus gave us all six requests in a certain order for a reason. You'll discover that beginning your prayer with God-centered requests will truly meet your needs.

F O U R

First Things First

Hallowed be your name.
Matthew 6:9

▼

Idle conversations have often led to great ideas. Great discoveries. Great inventions. Great plans for spring break.

They were participating in the great American Friday night event: cruising "the strip." Their particular strip was a three-mile stretch between the Sonic and the Davis Funeral Home parking lot. At the moment, Dwayne, Brian, Jay, and Karl were cramped into Dwayne's aged Camaro behind a long line of adolescent-filled cars, waving frantically at girls they hadn't seen since school let out six hours earlier.

Their conversation had already run the gamut of girls, basketball teams, the rumors about Bill and Sonja, and girls (again). It was during the momentary lull in conversation that Karl came up with The Plan.

"Spring break's coming," Karl began. "We ought to do something."

"Brilliant idea, Sherlock. 'We ought to do something.'" replied Dwayne.

"No, I mean it," continued Karl. "Get out of town. Go someplace we've never been. Do something we've never done before."

"Ever been white-water rafting?" asked Brian.

"Colorado!" said Jay.

"Padre Island!" shouted Dwayne.

"So, are you guys in?" All mumbled agreement with Karl's idea. "So let's make some plans for one unforgettable get-out-of-town spring break week!"

"What do you have in mind, Karl?" asked Dwayne.

Silence. "Do I have to think of everything?" asked Karl.

Jay said, "I think we should decide where we want to go first . . ."

"Like Padre Island," interrupted Dwayne.

"Like Colorado," continued Jay, "and then decide what we want to do when we get there."

"It would be better to decide what we want to do first, and then decide where we want to go to do it," said Dwayne.

"We may want to figure up how much money we have first, and see what we can afford," said Karl.

"There's one thing you're forgetting," replied Brian. "We might want to ask our parents first."

"Naw, let's make our plans first, get real organized. Show we can be responsible in planning a mature, safe, educational, well-budgeted, well-planned excursion, and our parents will be so impressed with our foresight that they will realize we are mature young men and naturally let us go," responded Karl, putting on his best Eddie Haskell be-polite-to-grownups voice.

It was obvious they weren't in agreement on how to plan, so Brian asked, "What are we going to do?"

The Camaro filled with four voices at once.

▼

A Chinese proverb states that a thousand miles begins with but a single step. But in what direction do you take that first step?

How do you begin a prayer? Does it matter? Just as the first steps four guys take in planning a trip will affect the whole of the trip, the first steps we take in prayer will affect the whole of our prayer. That's why Jesus taught us to begin our prayers with "Hallowed be your name." This is the most important part of all our prayers. It also may be the hardest to understand.

What in the World Is "Hallowed"?

Hallowed is not a word we hear in everyday conversation. When was the last time you heard someone use the word? *Hallowed* comes from the same word from which we get *holy*. To hallow something means to make it holy or set it apart as holy. In other words, to hallow God's name means to make God's name holy or to set God's name apart as holy.

But can I make God's name any holier than it already is? No.

> There is no one holy like the Lord; there is no one besides you; there is no Rock like our God.
>
> 1 Samuel 2:2

I am not praying that God would be more holy or that His name would become holier. God is God, and there is nothing I can do to add to or take away from His holiness. God is holy. Period.

But let's back up a minute and think about what exactly it means to be holy. What comes to mind when you think of someone who is holy?

A monk buried in a remote monastery who does nothing but think about God all day? A "saintly" grandmother who knits and prays for missionaries all day? Someone who does not allow herself to be touched in any way by the world around her? Unfortunately, the idea of holiness often brings up images of people out of touch with the real world. But that's not holiness.

Being *holy* simply means being separate or unique. Do you know who on this earth is holy? *Anyone who is a Christian.* If you are a Christian, then you are holy. You are set apart and different from others around you.

> But just as he who called you is holy, so be holy in all you do.
>
> 1 Peter 1:15

God has set the Christian apart from non-Christians. Jesus Christ personally lives in the hearts of Christians, and that makes them unique from the world around them. The world ought to see that Jesus has made a difference in Christians' lives. Not weird, just different.

So how is God holy? God is unique. God is set apart and distinct from everything around Him. The Creator is distinct from His creation.

When we say that God is holy, we are saying, "God, there is no one else like You. You are so far above everything else that no one can confuse you with anybody—or anything—else. You are unique from man because You understand all. You are set apart from man and his sinfulness because You have never sinned. God, You are completely distinct and unique from man and all creation. *You are holy.*"

How Do You Hallow Anything?

We still haven't answered the question, though: If God is so completely and perfectly holy, how can I hallow His name or make His name any holier? The first request in the Model Prayer, "Hallowed be your name," is not a prayer that God's name would be *more* holy, but that His name would be *recognized* as holy. We are asking God to work in such a way that it will be obvious that God is at work. We don't want people to notice us, we want people to notice God.

> "Hallowed be your name" is a prayer that His name be recognized as holy.

That's why this request is the very first request in the Model Prayer. Everything we do, everything we say, everything we think, everything we ask of God in prayer should have as its foundation this thought: *Does this honor God?* We should pray this request before we pray for anything else because all of our other requests should only be requests that honor God.

We pray, "Hallowed be your name," before we pray, "Give us today our daily bread [or other things we need]," because God's name will not be honored and hallowed if we misuse the things He gives us. Why should God give us the things we ask for if we're only going to use them in a way that does not honor Him? "When you ask, you do not receive, because you ask with wrong motives, that you may spend what you get on your pleasures" (James 4:3).

Why God Doesn't Answer All My Prayers
(Like I Think He Ought To)

Jesus gave us a wonderful promise concerning prayer: "You may ask me for anything in my name, and I will do it" (John 14:14).

A lot of people think that because Jesus said we may ask for anything, we can ask for *anything*. They reduce prayer to a magical formula: ask for it *in Jesus' name* and it's yours. Say "Abracadabra," and—poof!—whatever you want is there!

Why is this wrong? First of all, these folks greatly misunderstand what it means to pray in Jesus' name (we'll get into that later), but they also overlook the preceding verse: "And I will do whatever you ask in my name, so that the Son may bring glory to the Father" (John 14:13).

Read that again: "so that the Son may bring glory to the Father." Jesus wants to do incredible things in our lives. He wants us to have everything we need to experience a full and abundant life. But He will only do it in a way that will bring glory to the Father. Jesus is saying, "Ask anything of me and I will do it, and I will do it in such a way that my Father's name will be hallowed and honored."

I ask a lot of things of God that don't get answered. Actually, God answers *all* my prayers, but He doesn't answer them all in the way *I* want them answered. That's because Jesus didn't say He would do just anything we ask, but that He would do anything that brings glory to the Father. If God doesn't answer my prayer the way I want it answered, it's because I am asking for something that would not honor Him. Or perhaps the *way* I was asking was not honoring Him.

What's in a Name?

How can I know if what I am doing or asking is something that hallows and honors God's name? Is there some yardstick by which I can measure my life and requests so that I know that God is honored? Yes, there is, but to better understand it, we need to know something about names.

▼

Peter O'Neal stumbled through the front door, managing to drop only two of the packages in his overfilled arms. He and his wife, Rose, were expecting their first child within a few weeks, and they had been out shopping for the big event. The nursery furniture was all in place, and hopefully, with this last shopping trip, all the essentials were in place.

"Let's see, we've got the baby's diapers, the pajamas, the baby's, uh, things you wipe with," recounted Peter as he unsacked the goods in the nursery.

"There's one thing we still need to get for the baby," said Rose.

"What's that?" groaned Peter.

"A name. It's always the baby's this or the baby's that. We can't always call her . . ."

"Him," interrupted Peter.

"Or him 'the baby.'"

"Okay, let's do it. I remember buying a baby book, one of those 'Six Million Names for Your Baby' books."

Rose laughed as she pulled the book from a pile of Dr. Seuss books on the nursery bookshelf. "Have you looked at this book? It's written in . . . ," she opened the front cover, " . . . Scandinavian!"

Peter laughed. "That explains the great price."

"You and your bargains. Our baby's got an Irish last name and we want to call him . . . Olaf?"

Peter smiled. "Works for me." He took his wife's stare seriously. "Okay, okay, what do you suggest?"

▼

Any couple expecting a new baby, like the O'Neals, have a big task before them—choosing a name for their child. It's got to be the right name because, after all, it's going to be his or her name throughout his or her entire life.

In the time of the Bible, names were chosen for a different reason. Names were chosen because of their meaning. Persons' names had meaning and significance and were to be reflections of their personalities. For instance, one woman in the Old Testament, Hannah, prayed and prayed for a child. When God answered her prayer and gave her a son, she named him Samuel, which means *heard from God.*

Her son was a living testimony that God heard her prayer and gave her a son. Samuel carried that name—and lived up to its meaning—throughout his life. As an adult, Samuel served as judge for the nation of Israel, giving the people guidance from God and lifting the people up in his prayers to God. Samuel prayed and heard from God throughout his whole life.

Simon the fisherman became Peter at Jesus' command. Peter means *rock,* which seems ironic because Simon Peter was anything but a rock. Peter was always boasting or being a coward. He had the bad habit of putting his foot in his mouth. He had anything but the stability of a rock. But Jesus called him a rock to reflect the character of the man he would grow to become. Read about Peter in the Book of Acts or read the two letters that carry his name and you'll see someone who was rock solid. Jesus knew the potential in Peter and named him accordingly.

We may not change people's legal names today to reflect their character, but we do it in another way—nicknames. Nicknames are sometimes given in derision and mockery (Four Eyes, Pee Wee), sometimes as a name of fondness reflecting how others feel about that person (Honey, Sugar, Princess), and sometimes they're just descriptive (Curly, Red). Nicknames tell us something about the character of a person and how others view them.

Our names are important to us. Even if your name's meaning does not reflect your character, it represents *you.*

When someone talks about John Smith, they don't say something like, "I was talking the other day with the tall brown-haired male who plays trumpet in the band and is currently dating . . . ." No, they just use the name John Smith, and that name includes all the aspects of who John Smith is and what he does.

Let's think about God's name. That name represents who He is and what He does. The name is made up of only a few vowels and consonants. But, boy, what that name represents! God's name represents awesome power, infinite knowledge, measureless love and forgiveness, absolute holiness, and flawless guidance.

Every aspect of God's personality and character is summed up in His name. Therefore, when we pray for God's name to be hallowed and honored; we are praying that everything about God, everything that His name represents, would be honored.

▼

"Miss Alderson, please come to the seventh floor."

Janet nervously replaced the receiver. The seventh floor! That was the highest floor, the floor with all the fancy offices. The vice-presidents, senior vice-presidents, and the president. *What have I done now?* she wondered.

Janet made her way quickly to the elevator and the seventh floor. She walked through the glass doors emblazoned with the corporate logo, and told the secretary, "I'm . . . I'm Janet Alderson. I was told to . . ."

"Yes, Miss Alderson. Mr. Finch would like to speak with you," replied the receptionist.

Mr. Finch! Janet's mind was racing. *What would the president of this huge company want with a file clerk?*

Janet was ushered into Mr. Finch's office. Janet felt her shoes sink into the deep royal blue carpet. She looked around at the expansive office nervously. Rich, cherry paneling could be seen between framed diplomas, honorary degrees and expensive art pieces. A knight's suit of armor stood guard in front of one wall of leather-bound books.

"Miss Alderson, I'm William Finch." Janet's gaze turned quickly to the man addressing her. He was not tall, but he was impressive in his grey silk suit. He *looked* like a president.

"Please, have a seat," said Mr. Finch. His tone of voice was kind, and his mannerisms immediately put Janet at ease. He continued, "Miss Alderson, I've heard good reports about you. I've kept my eye on your progress in the company, and I'm pleased with what I hear. I believe you're just the person for the job. I'm going out of the country for awhile, and while I'm gone I want you to take care of my business."

This was crazy. "Your business?" asked Janet with a look of disbelief.

"My personal business," Mr. Finch continued, as though this was an everyday type of offer. "While I am gone, you will have the full use of my bank account and credit cards. I will give you power of attorney to conduct business in my name. You will be able to sign my name on any check and the bank will honor it."

Janet's mind was racing. *Mr. Finch was not a billionaire, but he was close!* Janet thought of all the things a person could do with that much money!

"I will pay you well and you will live well."

Janet's heart was pounding.

"But remember, Miss Alderson, it is my business and my money. You will represent me, so only spend money the way *I* would spend money. I trust you. And don't worry, you will be well rewarded."

The ringing of the telephone startled Janet. She came out of her daze and picked up the telephone receiver from her cluttered file clerk's desk.

"Miss Alderson, please come to the seventh floor," said the anonymous voice on the other end, "and pick up some more files."

Praying in Jesus' Name

Wouldn't it be great to have the use of a millionaire's bank account? But the truth is that we have been given an even greater opportunity. But it's not from some millionaire. It's not even from a *billionaire*. It's from God Himself.

> "My Father will give you whatever you ask in my name. Until now you have not asked for anything in my name. Ask and you will receive, and your joy will be complete."
>
> John 16:23–24

Jesus has given all Christians the privilege of praying in His name. They can ask any request of God as though it were Jesus Himself asking that request. Remember, though, it's *His* name. To pray and ask in Jesus' name means to pray and ask in a way that is consistent with what His name represents. Is this the kind of prayer Jesus would pray?

Christians can ask any request of God as though it were Jesus Himself asking that request

When we pray in a way that is consistent with Jesus' name and character—His love, compassion, and desire to please the Father—our prayers will always honor the name and character of God.

On Earth as It Is in Heaven

"Our Father in heaven, hallowed be your name, your kingdom come, your will be done on earth as it is in heaven." Notice that little phrase "on earth as it is in heaven." That phrase belongs with the first three requests.

Hallowed be your name—*on earth as it is in heaven.*
Your kingdom come—*on earth as it is in heaven.*
Your will be done—*on earth as it is in heaven.*

We are praying that God's name would be honored on earth as much as it is honored in heaven. Don't you think that God is completely honored and hallowed in heaven? Check out Revelation 4 and 5. You'll see a picture of the throne room of heaven where God in all His majesty sits. You'll read a description of the amazing beings that surround God's throne. It says about them:

Day and night they never stop saying:

"Holy, holy, holy
is the Lord God Almighty,
who was, and is, and is to come."

Whenever the living creatures give glory, honor and thanks to Him who sits on the throne and who lives for ever and ever, the twenty-four elders fall down before Him who sits on the throne, and worship Him who lives for ever and ever. They lay their crowns before the throne and say:

"You are worthy, our Lord and God,
to receive glory and honor and power,
for you created all things,
and by your will they were created
and have their being."

Revelation 4:8–11

When we pray "Hallowed be your name . . . on earth as it is in heaven," we are praying that God's loving name and awesome character would receive just as much honor here on earth as it gets around His throne. Our desire should not be that God would be honored a little. Our desire should be that God would be completely honored and glorified. Whatever we ask, whatever we do, we want God to be seen and glorified.

This request is first in the Model Prayer for a good reason: God's honor and glory come first. God first, me second. If I make this request first, all my other requests will receive the answer I desire, because I am asking for things that will honor Him.

▼

A C T S
—Responding to What I Read—

Adoration. Praise God for his uniqueness and holiness. Think about ways God is different from human beings and the rest of His creation. Praise Him because of His holy character. Praise Him because there is no one like God, no one who can perform miracles and do the mighty things He can do. Only He can answer your prayers.

Confession. If there have been times you have prayed for things just to satisfy your greed or desire for things, admit that to God. If your prayers for others are based more on your own convenience or well-being ("God, save that person so that they'll be nicer to me.") than on the concern that God be glorified in his or her life, admit that to God.

Thanksgiving. Thank God for the privilege of praying in His name. Thank Him for the trust He has placed in you and the opportunity to use His name and pray just as Jesus would pray.

Supplication. Is there something you need? Ask God to supply that need, but pray first that God would be honored in the thing He provides.

If you need direction or guidance about a decision you are facing, ask God to lead you to do the thing that will bring Him the most honor. If you are praying for a friend, ask God to work in your friend's life in a way that would bring that friend closer to Christ. When your friends are brought closer to Christ, God is always glorified.

Make a list of things about which you want to pray. For example:

▼ A big test

▼ A job interview

▼ Not getting along with a family member

▼ A friend who is lost

Take these requests and include them in a prayer that God's name would be hallowed.

"Lord, help me with this final exam today. Help me to think clearly and remember what I've learned. As a Christian, I want always to do my best. Guide me in doing my best. I want to give my all for You, that You would be pleased."

"I would really like this job, Lord. Help me to give a good first impression at the job interview. May Your light and love shine through me. I want this job, but I also want to honor You, Lord. Let me have this job only if I can be a witness for You among the people with whom I work."

"I'm having a difficult time with my father right now. Father, I know you are not honored when I do not honor my earthly father. Help me to have self-control and not lose my temper. Help me to love my dad, even when he makes unfair demands of me. Lord, I want to honor You by doing what is right in relation to my dad."

"Karen needs You in her life, Lord. Lead her to see that You can make a difference in her life. Glorify Yourself, God, by working this miracle in her life. Lead her to worship You by committing her life to You. Work that miracle, Lord, so that others, too, would see a change in Karen's life—a change that can only be attributed to You."

Don't hesitate to ask God for things, but always ask for things in a way that would honor Him.

▼

F I V E

Better Than the Magic Kingdom

Your kingdom come.
Matthew 6:9

▼

Julia St. James spent two weeks last summer with ten other juniors and seniors on Mrs. Austin's annual tour of the United Kingdom.

Lisa Fillmore took a summer trip with her family to Orlando, Florida to visit the Magic Kingdom.

Mary Jenson worked all summer as a tour guide at the new children's museum. She gave children tours of the Plant and Animal Kingdom.

So what do you think came to their minds when they were asked the question during their Sunday morning Bible study, "What does the kingdom of God look like?"

Julia pictured stately Beefeaters in red coats and black hats, looking terribly somber. Mickey, Goofy, and seven dwarfs kept popping into Lisa's head, and Mary thought of *rosa odorata* and *equus burchelli.*

▼

What comes to your mind when you think of a kingdom?

It's an important question because it has to do with the second type of request Jesus told us to pray: "Your kingdom come." It's the shortest request, but don't let its shortness fool you—it packs a lot of punch. We don't always see the "punch," though, because we don't fully understand the idea of a *kingdom.*

What Is a Kingdom?

In America we elect those who lead our government. We choose who will lead us and we place them in office to make laws and enforce them, but we have also limited their power to keep them from becoming dictators.

The United States government has a system of checks and balances so that no one person or group has too much control. If we don't like the way they are handling our government or leading us, then we can choose not to reelect them.

A kingdom, though, runs by a different set of rules. In a kingdom, the king is *the* ruler. What he says goes, and he is the king for life. The king has all the authority and gives all the commands, period.

Look at the kings of Israel in the Old Testament. With the exception of Saul, the first king, all the kings were ancestors of David. There were no elections; a certain person was king because it was his place in the family tree. This didn't automatically make them good kings. Many of them abused their powers. Because they were kings, they set the pace for the rest of the kingdom.

King Josiah led the nation to return to God and experience revival. But King Manasseh led the nation to abandon God and travel down a destructive path. How could he do this? Because he was the king. People followed him simply because he was the ruler.

When Jesus first taught His disciples this prayer, "Your kingdom come," the disciples knew of a different kind of king. They lived in the Roman Empire. The emperors of the Roman Empire often ruled with an iron hand and considered themselves above the law.

What kind of ruler was the Roman emperor? If a Roman senator failed to respond immediately to a letter from Caesar, he could be put to death. If the senator even laughed or smiled at the wrong time, it could mean his death. The emperor Tiberius not only had the right to raise taxes and declare war or peace, but to investigate people's private lives. He could condemn anyone if he disapproved of that person's morals or lifestyle.

The emperor did as he chose, interfered in the private business of anyone he chose, and dictated the morals of any group or individual at his own whim. Yet, he himself was above the law. The Roman emperor went beyond the normal dictates of a king; *he made himself god.*

The Difference of God's Kingdom

The disciples clearly understood that living in someone's kingdom meant living according to the rules and laws of that king. But Jesus wasn't talking to them about any ordinary king. He was talking about God the Father. God the Father loves, protects, cares, calms fears, gives hope, builds confidence and is always there. Do you see what that means? God does not rule harshly or hatefully; His rule over us is seasoned with love.

For those who live in His kingdom, God will protect them from harm. He is also a King who is approachable at any time. He is involved with those in His kingdom and cares about their quality of life. The emperors cared about the quality of their *own* lives, but God cares for the quality of life for everybody.

God's kingdom is still a kingdom, though. It is still a place where the king is in complete charge. But for those who are willing to live under the kingship of God and surrender their wills to His, the kingdom is a place of joyful living.

God's kingdom is a place where the King is in complete charge.

It's too bad most people reject Jesus' idea of a kingdom. Can man's earthly kingdoms compare with these characteristics?

> The kingdom of God is not a matter of eating and drinking, but of righteousness, peace and joy in the Holy Spirit.
> Romans 14:17

> The kingdom of God is not a matter of talk but of power.
> 1 Corinthians 4:20

Here's the best part: this righteousness, peace, joy and power go on ... forever! Hebrews 12:28 tells us that God's kingdom is a kingdom that cannot be shaken. Can any world government make that claim? There have been many great world empires throughout history, but they were all eventually shaken and destroyed. Man's kingdoms never last; God's kingdom lasts forever.

How Does His Kingdom Come?

God's kingdom is sounding better and better, isn't it? I want to live in a place where God is in such control that life's frustrations are gone and I can live peacefully and contented. No hassles, no heartache, no pain. I want that kind of kingdom.

But wait a minute. Just exactly *how* does His kingdom come? If Jesus gave this prayer request to His disciples almost two thousand years ago and His followers have been praying this request for almost two thousand years, then why hasn't His kingdom come?

But His kingdom has come! At least, partially, anyway. You see, there are two stages to the coming of God's kingdom. Let's look at these two stages and we will see exactly *how* His kingdom comes.

Stage #1: Jesus Is Lord of My Life

When we become Christians, we turn from our sins and old ways, look to Jesus Christ for forgiveness, and ask Him to come into our lives and make us new. In one sense, it's really quite simple. A simple prayer of trust.

It is simple, but it will cost us. It will cost us everything. "If you confess with your mouth, 'Jesus is Lord,' and believe in your heart that God raised him from the dead, you will be saved" (Romans 10:9). Salvation comes when we confess Jesus is Lord. Confessing is more than just uttering words; it is admitting something that we know is true and choosing to live our lives in a way that conforms to that truth. It is one thing to *say*, "Jesus is Lord." It is quite another thing to *live* "Jesus is Lord."

Lord is another one of those words that has lost some of its meaning in our modern do-your-own-thing life-styles. A lord is someone who has authority and power. When you acknowledge someone as lord, you are accepting his authority and power.

▼

Nelson was not having a good day at work. The owner and manager of the Burger Barn, Mr. Ferguson, would not ease up on him. Or so it seemed to Nelson.

Nelson had begun his work day by asking Mr. Ferguson for next Saturday off. All Nelson's friends—the ones who didn't have to work—were heading for the beach. But Ferguson said no. Never mind that the weather was warming up and this was the first chance they had to go to the beach since last September. Mr. Ferguson said no. He needed Nelson on Saturday.

At the moment, Nelson was fuming over his lost Saturday while he cleaned the restrooms. Why was he cleaning the restrooms? Because Mr. Ferguson *said* to clean the restrooms. He was fishing out a roll of toilet paper that some kid "accidentally" dropped into the toilet, when Mr. Ferguson opened the door.

"Nelson?" Mr. Ferguson asked, unable to see Nelson warily holding a soaking wet roll of toilet paper in the back stall.

"Yes, sir?"

"There's a spilt milkshake by the front door. Clean it up. And empty the trash cans while you're at it."

Nelson was tempted to say, "No, thanks, I'd rather not. I'm having too much fun back here. This is more fun than the beach," but he held his tongue. In this small town, the Burger Barn was the only place he could get a job, and he didn't want to lose it over some sarcastic remark.

He knew what he had to do if he wanted to get his paycheck from Mr. Ferguson. He washed the little pieces of wet toilet paper off his hands, grabbed the mop and went to tackle the milkshake.

Nelson's boss at the Burger Barn is something like a lord. He has authority and power, and if Nelson wants to keep that job, he will accept Mr. Ferguson as boss and submit to his authority and power. But Mr. Ferguson's authority is limited. He can't tell Nelson to do his homework. He can't make Nelson do his chores at home. Mr. Ferguson's authority is limited to the Burger Barn. As long as Nelson is working at the Burger Barn, Mr. Ferguson is the boss. But when Nelson punches out at the time clock and leaves the parking lot, he is on his own.

▼

To become Christians, we must accept Jesus into our lives as Lord. The Boss. He is not just Lord on Sunday mornings. He is not just the Boss when we read the Bible or pray. He is Lord *all the time.*

If we're honest, though, Jesus isn't always Lord of our lives. There are times when we call the shots in our lives, doing things our way. We may know Him to be the King, but we are not actively letting Him *be* the King. Becoming a Christian is a one-time event. We give our lives to Christ and, in that instant, we become new creations. In one initial act, we give the control—the lordship—of our lives to Christ. *But that initial act must be actively practiced in our lives every day.*

Marriage might be a good illustration. My marriage began with one initial, decisive act: a wedding. My wife and I made a commitment to each other and now we are husband and wife. Day-to-day circumstances do not change the fact that I am married. But for my marriage to be good and strong, I must daily act in a manner that confirms that I have a wife for whom I love and care. I proudly wear a wedding ring that symbolizes my commitment. I don't date other women. I look for ways to please my wife. I don't get "remarried" every day, but I daily act in a way that shows I am married and affirms the commitment I made at our wedding.

That's what Christians should do daily. "But in your hearts set apart Christ as Lord" (1 Peter 3:15). This passage means we are *continually* to set apart Christ as Lord, daily surrendering our wants and desires to the will of our King, Jesus.

> We give the control—the lordship—of our lives to Christ. But that initial act must be actively practiced in our lives every day.

The first request was that God's name would be hallowed and honored. The request, "Your kingdom come," aptly follows because there is no better way for God to be honored than for Him to be recognized as Lord and King. When I allow Him to be fully King in my life, He is honored.

We can also pray this prayer in another way. "God, I ask that your kingdom would come into the life of my friend." This is a request that others would find Christ, that others would give themselves over to the rule and reign of Christ. God's kingdom is absent in many hearts and we should pray for the salvation of others: friends, family members, even enemies.

Stage #2: The Physical Return of Christ

So far, we have only considered the coming of God's kingdom in an internal, invisible sense. We let Him be Lord, and His kingdom is revealed in the way we let Jesus shine through us. But God's kingdom will not always be just a kingdom within our hearts. Jesus has promised that He will return someday and set up His kingdom—a physical kingdom—on earth.

> For the Lord himself will come down from heaven, with a loud command, with the voice of the archangel and with the trumpet call of God, and the dead in Christ will rise first. After that, we who are still alive and are left will be caught up with them in the clouds to meet the Lord in the air. And so we will be with the Lord forever.
>
> 1 Thessalonians 4:16–17

> And you will receive a rich welcome into the eternal kingdom of our Lord and Savior Jesus Christ.
>
> 2 Peter 1:11

Though God's kingdom can be on earth now within our own lives, we still must live in a hostile, imperfect world. But when Jesus returns, there will be peace not only within our hearts, but throughout society. Danger and crime will disappear. Poverty will be overcome by security, contentment and happiness. God's kingdom will be the best of everything—with no drawbacks. God will be completely free to reign as He chooses, and because of His great love for us, His kingdom will be an incredible, perfect place!

▼

Nelson wrung out the mop one last time. The spilt milkshake was gone, at least until the next time a small child ordered a chocolate milkshake.

He surveyed the eating area. No small children. Only a small band of senior citizens huddled around their coffee cups and two kids from school talking and fighting over French fries. *I wish I could sit and laugh and eat fries*, thought Nelson as he carried the mop and bucket to the back, *instead of having to clean them up.*

Mark and Sean were doing more than fighting over French fries. Mark was giving his assessment of life in general. "This week is the pits," he said, "My term paper is due, the physics experiment is due, I've got rehearsals for the play, my girlfriend is mad at me, my parents are mad at me. . . . I hate all this pressure. I have too much to do, and too little time to do it. And I don't feel like doing anything because everyone is mad at me."

There was a pause as Sean slurped the remains of his drink. "Someday this will be behind you. Jesus will return and take you away from all this," Sean said casually.

Mark thought on that for awhile, remembering the study Sean and he had been doing at church. "Would be nice. I'm ready for Jesus to come back and remove me from all these hassles."

"Gee, Mark, I didn't mean *right now.*"

"Why not? Think about it. Everything we hate, everything bad, will be gone. It will be a perfect life. This world and my life would both be better if Jesus came back today."

Mark's seriousness was a sharp contrast to Sean's casual, almost flippant attitude. It made Sean uncomfortable. "Well, gee, Mark, I . . . sure I want Jesus to return, but I wouldn't mind if He waited a bit. This life isn't *that* bad. I want Jesus to return but I also want to date, get out on my own, go to college, get married. I've still got my whole life ahead of me!"

▼

Sean's response is perfectly natural for a young person with most of life still waiting to be experienced. But as good as this life can be, it won't compare to the life God has waiting for us! Imagine the best possible life in the best possible place with the best possible joys and thrills, and God will go way beyond even that.

> No eye has seen, no ear has heard, no mind has conceived what God has prepared for those who love him.
>
> 1 Corinthians 2:9

We can't even *imagine* how great God's kingdom will be. We can only look forward to it with anticipation. We should enjoy the life God has given us now, do our best in all that we do, and make the most of what we've got in this life. But we need to remember: the return of Jesus will bring us into an incredible kingdom that will outshine anything this world has to offer.

On Earth as It Is in Heaven

We are to pray "Your kingdom come . . . on earth as it is in heaven." Heaven is the center of God's kingdom and His throne is there. Imagine what such a perfect kingdom would be like. All residents of heaven are there because they choose to be there and submit gladly to God's royal reign and control. Because God has complete reign in heaven, it is a place of complete happiness, security and love.

Wouldn't it be great if earth was under God's reign and control like heaven is? God knows what is best for all of us and He would be free to work His power and love on our behalf. That should motivate us to pray, "God, bring all the beauty, awesomeness, and power of Your kingdom down to earth, so that earth will be like heaven. And while I'm waiting for You to set that kingdom up on earth, set it up in my life. Reign in my life and take complete control. No matter what the world does around me, You are my King. What You say goes. Jesus, be King on earth . . . just like You are King in heaven."

▼

A C T S
—Responding to What I Read—

Adoration. Praise God for being the perfect King. Praise Him because He is an unshakable, powerful, yet loving King. Praise Him for being King of kings and Lord of lords.

Confession. We all have times in our lives when we choose to do things our way. It is a sin, though, when we don't allow Jesus to be Lord and have full control of our lives. Is Jesus Lord (Boss) of your . . .

   . . . family relationships?
   . . . dating and social life?
   . . . school work and activities?
   . . . plans for the future?

Confess to God those times when you didn't let Him work in your life. As you confess, ask Him to make you aware of when you're in control of your life as opposed to when He is in control.

Thanksgiving. Thank God for saving you and making you a new creation, a part of His kingdom. Thank Him for coming into your life as Savior, Lord, and King.

Supplication. First, ask Jesus to be Lord of your life. Acknowledge Him as the Master of your life and surrender your will to His will.

Second, pray for a friend or family member. Is there someone you are close to who does not know Christ? Do you know a Christian who is not living a Christ-controlled life? Ask God to work in that person's life so that he, too, will surrender his life to God.

Third, pray that Jesus would return soon and set up His earthly kingdom. Ask God to help you remember the words of Philippians 3:20: "But our citizenship is in heaven. And we eagerly await a Savior from there, the Lord Jesus Christ, who, by the power that enables Him to bring everything under His control, will transform our lowly bodies so that they will be like His glorious body."

▼

S I X

Have It Your Way

Your will be done.
Matthew 6:10

▼

Barry wanted to go out of state and study engineering, while Sheryl had a basketball scholarship at the local college. There was one snag in their plans: Barry and Sheryl were also in love and wanted to get married. They sat at their usual corner table at The Taco Factory one Friday night discussing their dilemma.

"Are you sure you want to go so far away?" asked Sheryl again.

"It's the best school. I've been accepted. I can't let this slip by," replied Barry. "But you could . . ."

Sheryl stopped him. "We've been over that, too. I can't let such a good scholarship go by."

The conversation stopped as the waiter set four soft tacos and two soft drinks in front of them. But Barry and Sheryl did not pick up their food immediately.

"What do you think God wants us to do?" asked Barry.

Sheryl replied with her own question. "You believe God wants us to get married . . . don't you?"

Barry's mind raced. He thought of all the conversations he had had with others on this same subject.

Brad, his youth minister: "God's will? We know God's will calls for us to obey our parents. What do your parents have to say about the matter?"

Dad: "Barry, marriage is out of the question. It could jeopardize your college education and, besides, you're too young."

Mom (to Dad): "Now, Jim, don't forget. You were his age when we got married . . . and you've done just fine."

Dan, his best friend: "God's will? Don't worry about it. God's going to do what He wants to anyway. Just make your plans and do what you want to do. It's all fate. Predetermined fate."

Barry wasn't sure how to answer his girlfriend. "Well . . . uh . . . I think so. I want God's will to be done. I just wish I knew what God's will is."

Barry's on the right track. No matter what the outcome, he wants God's will to be done. That's what the Model Prayer has been leading to.

We began our prayer with the request that God's name be honored. This first request naturally leads into the second request, because where is God's name more honored than in the place where He is allowed to reign as King? And in the kingdom, where God is allowed to be fully King, His will prevails. This, then, leads to the third request: "Your will be done."

Let's ask the same question Barry asked: How can I make sure God's will is being done in my life? To answer that, though, we must ask a more basic question.

What Exactly Is God's Will?

Everybody has a will: wants, desires, inclinations. We make all our decisions based on our will, desires and preferences. For instance, you made a choice this morning to get out of bed—and that may have been a hard decision! You may have wanted to sleep a little longer, but your desire not to be absent or fail school was greater! You make decisions every day: to wear certain clothes, to watch a certain program, to play a certain game.

Some of our willful choices are easy: what to eat, what homework to do first, who to call. Other choices are out of our hands. We may have a strong desire to play professional basketball, but other than practicing hard and doing our best, we can't force ourselves into the NBA just because we want it. Or we may want to drive a Ferrari, but just *wanting* one doesn't mean we'll *get* one.

God has wants and desires, too. The big difference between God and us is that God can do something about His desires. When God wants to do something, He does it. Take the story of creation. God wanted light so He said, "Let there be light." And there it was! "You are worthy, our Lord and God, to receive glory and honor and power, for you created all things, and *by your will* they were created and have their being" (Revelation 4:11). Just by saying the word, God accomplished His will in creation.

If It's God's Will, Won't He Do It Anyway?

God is all-powerful—He can do anything He wants.
God is all-knowing—He always knows what's best.
God is all-loving—He will only do what is best.

If these statements are true—and they are—then doesn't God automatically do what He wants to do? He knows what is best, so does it matter what I pray?

Yes, it is true that there are things that God does—no matter what. It's His will to do those things, and He's going to do them. Period.

> I form the light and create darkness, I bring prosperity and create disaster; I, the LORD, do all these things.
>
> Woe to him who quarrels with his Maker, to him who is but a potsherd among the potsherds on the ground. Does the clay say to the potter, 'What are you making?' Does your work say, 'He has no hands'?
>
> Isaiah 45:7,9

God can do anything He wills to do, but that does not take away from our privilege to pray. Even though there are things that God wills to do no matter what, there are many other ways that God does not force His will.

Remember: we all have wills and can make choices. If we could only do what *God* willed us to do, it wouldn't be our choice, would it? We would be like machines or robots. God has desires for each one of us but He will never force His desires on us. It's our choice.

Letting God's Will Be Done

There are two sides to God's will, then. One side is a *determined* matter: this *is* what God's going to do. Like creation—God determined to create the sun, moon and stars, and He did it. No one could stop Him.

But there's another side to God's will. It has to do with His *desires* for us. These plans are for our very best, but it is our choice whether we let that best be done in our lives. Here's a good example:

This is good, and pleases God our Savior, who wants all men to be saved and to come to a knowledge of the truth.

1 Timothy 2:3–4

In the same way your Father in heaven is not willing that any of these little ones should be lost.

Matthew 18:14

God's will is that no one die in his or her sins and go to hell; His will is that all people know Him and spend eternity with Him in heaven. But does everyone become a Christian? Does everyone go to heaven? Unfortunately, no. It is God's gracious design and aim that no one be lost, but it is up to each individual to choose God's plan of salvation.

When we pray "Your will be done," we are choosing God's will over our own. This is a prayer of surrender. Surrendering to the will of God does not take away our privilege to ask things of God. God *wants* us to ask great things of Him.

Call to me and I will answer you and tell you great and unsearchable things you do not know.

Jeremiah 33:3

Ask and it will be given to you; seek and you will find; knock and the door will be opened to you.

Matthew 7:7

Yes, we are free to ask, even commanded to ask, but surrendering to His will means accepting *His* answers. Jesus gives us the best example of someone accepting the Father's will and the Father's answers.

Were All Jesus' Prayers Answered?

Of course, Jesus' prayers were answered! He was the Son of God, wasn't He?! It does seem like a silly question, doesn't it? But before we lightly dismiss the question with a yes, simply because we are talking about Jesus, read carefully this prayer that Jesus prayed.

> He fell to the ground and prayed that if possible the hour might pass from him. "*Abba*, Father," he said, "everything is possible for you. Take this cup from me. Yet not what I will, but what you will."
> Mark 14: 35–36

Jesus prayed this prayer on the night before His death—the night when He was to be arrested, tried, mocked, beaten, spit upon, and finally killed. He knew what was before Him. After all, this was the reason Jesus gave up His glory in heaven and came to earth.

The human side of Jesus did not want to go through with it. Jesus was God, but He was also fully man. He had the same aversion to pain we all have. He was in deep anguish thinking about what He was going to go through. So He prayed, "*Abba*, Father, everything is possible for you. Take this cup from me."

Did His Father answer that one request? No, He didn't. I don't imagine Jesus had ever prayed any harder than He did that night, but His Father did not answer that one request, "Take this cup from me."

But Jesus' prayer didn't end there. As much as the human side of Jesus may have wanted to avoid the pain and death that were to come, He prayed further, "Yet not what I will, but what you will."

Jesus was willing to surrender His human desire to the greater desire of His Father. "For I have come down from heaven not to do my will but to do the will of him who sent me" (John 6:38). This attitude of submission permeated every part of Jesus' life.

So, in one sense, Jesus' one request wasn't answered, but His ultimate, final prayer was answered. He laid His request before God and left it in His hands: "Yet not what I will, but what you will."

Why God Doesn't "Answer" All Our Prayers

Have you ever known someone who lost faith in God because He didn't answer his or her prayer? Unfortunately, I have known too many.

There was Amanda, a high school girl whose grandmother was very sick. She prayed and prayed for her grandmother. She asked the youth group at church to pray for her grandmother. And they did. Did her grandmother miraculously recover? No, she got worse and finally died. Amanda's question was, "Why did God let my grandmother die?" She decided God didn't care; "If God was a God of love," she said, "He wouldn't have let this happen." Amanda drifted away from the church and from God.

> If God doesn't give us the specific thing we ask for, that means He has something even better in store for us.

The truth is that God does answer all our prayers, but many people get mad at God because He doesn't answer their prayers the way *they* want them answered. But if God doesn't give us the specific thing we ask for, that means that He has something even better in store for us.

Which of Jesus' requests would you have wanted God the Father to answer: "take this cup from me" or "your will be done?" God the Father didn't take the cup away from His Son because He had something better in store: our salvation. Removing the cup of pain and death from His Son would have saved Jesus, but it wouldn't have helped us at all. The pain and suffering for Jesus were only temporary; the victory and salvation for us were for eternity.

I'm glad God doesn't answer all my prayers the way I want them answered. I look back on earlier times in my life when God said no to some of my prayer requests. I didn't understand why at the time, but I can look back now and see that the answer God did give me was far better than what I had initially asked for.

In the beginning years of my work with students, I had a student named Kenneth who had been dating this one girl for a long time, and he was sure that this was the girl God wanted him to marry.

But one day they broke up. Kenneth was shaken. "If we weren't meant for each other, then why did God bring us together? I was sure she was the only one for me."

I said, "Kenneth, God may have wanted to teach both of you about relationships and about the kind of person you will ultimately marry. And as much as you thought she was the perfect girl for you, thank God that it didn't work out."

"Why should I thank God for a thing like that?"

"Because that means—as much as you liked her—God's got someone even better in store for you!"

Kenneth smiled at that thought. And it was true. Now, years later, Kenneth is happily married and has a great relationship with the wife God knew all along he should marry. God didn't just give Kenneth what was good, He gave Kenneth what was best for him.

God wants to do the same thing for all of us. He doesn't want just to give us *good* things; He wants to give us the *best* things. So the next time we don't receive what we have asked for in prayer, we should thank God and trust Him. He's got something even better in store for us.

Should I Just Pray Vague Prayers, Then?

So I should just pray, "God, You know what's best, so You do as You want." Seems logical, doesn't it?

This would be true except for one remarkable fact: God doesn't want just to do things for us; He wants us to participate with Him in His kingdom's work. He wants to work *with* us and *through* us. This brings Him greater honor; our spontaneous response is to thank Him and praise Him when we see Him do something that we know He did and we didn't. And we receive an incredible sense of joy because we know we were a part of God's work.

If we only pray in vague ways—"God, do whatever You want in this matter"—how will we know if He answers? When I was a boy, I prayed the UVP (Ultimate Vague Prayer). During my nightly bedtime prayer, I always said, "God bless all the people in the world." It was a nice thought, but how was God to answer it? How did I want God to bless them? And how would I ever know if God *had* blessed all the people in the world?

We miss out when we pray vague prayers because we have no sense of being a part of God's ministry. Specific requests receive specific answers. Seeing God answer in definite ways gives us cause to be joyous and praise Him.

Praying Intelligently

Yes, we can ask things of God—definite, specific things—and receive definite, specific answers. "This is the assurance we have in approaching God: that if we ask anything according to His will, He hears us. And if we know that He hears us whatever we ask we know that we have what we asked of Him" (1 John 5:14–15). The secret to getting our prayers answered in a specific way is to pray according to God's will. Pray intelligently.

But How Can I Know God's Will?

If I'm to pray in agreement with God's will, how can I know God's will so that I can pray in agreement with it?! The first—and most obvious—answer is through the Bible. Through the Bible, God has revealed Himself to us so that we can know who He is, what He is like, and what His will is.

Is it God's will for someone to lie on a job application? No, because the Bible tells us plainly that God expects honesty and integrity from us at all times. Is it God's will for someone to steal something he needs? No, because God's Word tells us to honor the rights and possessions of others. God's Word contains God's will. In fact, everything we need to know to live according to God's will is right there in the Bible. Everything.

"Wait a minute? *Everything* I need to know? What about the details?! Should I attend this college or that college? Marry this person or that person? Wear this shirt or that shirt?"

I'll admit you won't find a verse in the Bible that states specifically: "Thou shalt marry Clarence when thou reachest the age of two score and four years." The commands and principles presented in the Bible all have to do with God's will for our character. But as we follow God's will for our character, we'll discover that more and more of the details of our lives will fall into place. "But seek first his kingdom and his righteousness, and all these things will be given to you as well" (Matthew 6:33).

There are times, of course, when we need specific direction. "If any of you lacks wisdom, he should ask God, who gives generously to all without finding fault, and it will be given to him" (James 1:5).

How does God give us the wisdom we need to know His will? God will speak to us, and lead us through the counsel of other Christians, the circumstances in which we find ourselves, and even our own common sense.

Develop the discipline of thinking like God. Pursue the mind of Christ. "Do not conform any longer to the pattern of this world, but be transformed by the renewing of your mind. Then you will be able to test and approve what God's will is—his good, pleasing and perfect will" (Romans 12:2).

So spend time in the Bible. We should let the guidance of the Bible replace the world's way of thinking in our minds. The Bible will show us how God has worked in

the past and it will give us deep insights into His character and will. After all, the Bible is the mind of Christ.

Here's how studying the Bible and developing the
mind of Christ can help you make decisions and seek the
will of God: Suppose you are praying about a decision
and you have two choices. You would do well to see if
both choices are compatible with God's character. Could
one of these choices lead you to compromise your walk
with Christ? Will one of these choices bring greater glory
to God? Will one glorify you instead of God? As God's
Word fills our minds, we will begin to know—yes, even
test and approve—what God's will is.

On Earth as It Is in Heaven

There is no question that God reigns completely as King
in heaven, so that means His will is completely carried
out there. No sinful mistakes. No second-rate choices or
decisions. God's best is always carried out.

What would earth be like if God's ideal was always
carried out? Is crime, abuse, prejudice, or jealousy a part
of God's will? Of course not, so earth would be a place
where we all get along. No crime, abuse, prejudice, or
jealousy. Think of all the death and disease that would
be wiped out simply because we all followed God's best
for our lives. No AIDS, smoking-related lung problems,
crack babies, alcoholism, or drug abuse.

Our desire in prayer is that God's desires and plans
would be carried out right here on earth as thoroughly
and completely as they are in heaven. "Lord, let Your will
be done—and let it begin with me."

▼

A C T S
—Responding to What I Read—

Adoration. Praise God for being good and perfect. Praise Him for His care for us. He does have a special plan for each of us. Praise Him because His will for us is always good and perfect.

Confession. Have you been guilty of following your own plans and devices? Doing things your own way and then praying that God would bless your desires or efforts? If so, admit these things to God and surrender your plans in God's will. Let Him know that you intend to get to know Him more by spending time with Him in the Bible. If you are not spending time daily in the Bible, make a specific plan of action on how you will begin doing so.

Thanksgiving. Thank God for not leaving us alone to try and figure out His will. Thank God for giving us the Bible and showing us who He is through it. Thank God for the privilege of knowing Him intimately.

Supplication. Ask God to help you develop the mind of Christ. Ask Him to give you an understanding of the Bible so that you can know Him better. First Timothy 2:4 tells us that God "wants all men . . . to come to a knowledge of the truth." You can pray this confidently, because it is God's will.

▼

PART THREE

Now It's My Turn

▼

Have you noticed something about this book? We have yet to ask anything for ourselves! Yet that's how we usually begin our prayers. With our needs. With what we want. Personal requests are usually our starting point in prayer.

But Jesus placed God first. We are, first of all, to pray concerning His character, His kingdom and His will. God first; man second. This is not to say that God does not care about our needs. But it is only when we let God have first place in our hearts, lives, and prayers that He is able truly to meet our needs in the best way possible.

Let's consider the three areas Jesus tells us to pray about concerning ourselves.

S E V E N

Here's What I Need . . .

Give us today our daily bread.
Matthew 6:8

▼

Midway through the season, major league baseball came to a halt. The players went on strike. The issue? Money, of course. The players didn't think they were getting their fair share from the owners. A few players didn't think they were getting paid what they were worth. So they stopped America's pastime and went on strike.

Others weren't getting their paychecks either because of the strike. Victor Sanchez was an eighteen-year-old custodian in the Astrodome. As long as there was a baseball strike, Vic had no games to clean up after. Vic's education took a backseat when his mother became ill the previous year. The government helped, but Vic's mother and two brothers depended on Vic's job at the Dome.

Vic leaned against the kitchen counter and slowly ate a sandwich—processed American cheese pasted between two pieces of white bread from the day-old bakery. Over the sink hung an embroidered copy of the Lord's

Prayer. His mother had hung it there years ago and had taught it to all three of her sons.

As if by habit, Vic read the prayer. When he came to the line "Give us this day our daily bread," he looked at his half-eaten sandwich. *I guess I should thank the Lord that He has given me my daily bread,* Vic said to himself, *but right now I'd like a lot more.*

There are two obvious extremes in the story above. One extreme is to take the request, "Give us today our daily bread," and accept it at only its literal face value. It is the idea that we are entitled only to ask for bread for today, and expect nothing more. The other extreme is to move beyond our needs, demanding that all our extravagant desires be supplied. Vic doesn't think he has the right to ask for more than the barest necessities; the baseball players ask for too much.

God wants us to ask things of Him. He loves us and wants to meet our needs. In fact, He has given us that promise. "My God will meet all your needs according to his glorious riches in Christ Jesus" (Philippians 4:19).

It's important, though, that we know *how* to ask. With the fourth request in the Model Prayer, Jesus gives us just the right balance and shows us how to ask for physical things. Let's look beyond the surface and see what it means to pray, "Give us today our daily bread."

Just Bread? What About Pizza?

Daily bread signifies anything we need in order to live. Common sense tells us that we need three things to survive: food, clothing, shelter. But God is not just concerned that we survive, He wants us to experience *life!* So let's expand our list a bit:

▼ Food   ▼ Family
▼ Clothes   ▼ Friends
▼ Shelter   ▼ Education
▼ Home   ▼ Transportation
▼ Health   ▼ Employment

Jesus said, "I have come that they may have life, and have it to the full." Life with a capital L, not just existence. The difference between life and existence is like the difference between flour, eggs, sugar, milk, butter . . . and a cake! It's like the difference between a house and a home. We're not limited to asking God to provide a dry roof over our heads; we can ask Him to provide us with a good home life—a place where we feel secure and have a sense of fellowship and belonging.

Wants Versus Needs

We can look to God for everything we need to experience this full life, but I emphasize the word *need.* The things we *need* are quite often different from what we *want.*

Here's a desire that every sixteen year old deals with: an automobile. Transportation is a common need in our society. Home, school, and work may be separated by miles and we need some way to get around. We can pray for a friend to help us get around or pray that a parent will be free to get us where we need to go. And it's not wrong to ask God for some permanent transportation (our own car!).

It's okay to pray for a car. "Lord, I need a car to get to my job after school. I can't keep mooching from my friends or asking Mom to leave work to get me there."

Now listen to see if you hear the difference in *this* prayer: "Lord, I need a car. I know You can do anything and one car is the same as another to You. So why not make it one of those red Mazda Miata convertibles?" It's one thing to say what we need; it's another thing to say what we covet.

We should ask ourselves: *What is my motive in asking for this? Is it a need, or is it greed?* Be honest with yourself and God.

Honesty means not trying to hide our true motives behind spiritual pretense. See if you can tell the difference in these examples:

"God, I would like a raise at my job. You know, God, if I had more money, I could give more to the church."

"God, You've got to help me win that game this afternoon. Help me make every shot and free throw. If I could win that game, I'd be a hero, and I'd be in a really good position to witness to the rest of the team."

We must check our motives. In James 4:3 we read, "When you ask, you do not receive, because you ask with wrong motives, that you may spend what you get on your pleasures." God's desire is to meet our needs and help us with life, but He's not a Santa Claus who gives us unnecessary frills and thrills.

A Relationship of Dependence and Trust

Have you ever seen the Civil War movie *Shenandoah?* At the beginning of the story, the father, played by Jimmy

Stewart, sits down with his family for dinner. They bow their heads and Stewart offers this prayer: "Lord, we cleared this land. We plowed it, sowed it and harvested it. It wouldn't be here, we wouldn't be eatin' it, if we hadn't all done it ourselves. We worked dog-bone hard for every crumb and morsel, but we thank you just the same anyway, Lord, for the food we are about to eat."

There's truth in that prayer. Let's put it in a different context: *I* earned the money to buy the food; *I* am the one who went to the store to purchase the food; *I* am the one who slaved in the kitchen preparing the meal.

I may have done all that, but I'm still dependent upon God. The farmer and I are dependent upon God to provide good soil and good weather for the plants to grow. I am dependent upon God for my job or the money I need to buy food. No matter how we look at it, the bottom line is that we are still dependent upon God.

Our attitude in this reflects our relationship with God. Although God may not *directly* put food on my table, do I still recognize His role in the process and do I acknowledge my dependence on Him? Am I trusting myself or am I trusting God? "But remember the LORD your God, for it is he who gives you the ability to produce wealth" (Deuteronomy 8:18).

God wants us to recognize our dependence on Him for our physical needs, and He wants us to trust Him that He *will* meet those physical needs. Look at the request again: "Give us *today* our daily bread." We move beyond just saying we depend on God; we acknowledge that we trust Him to provide. God cares about us and He wants—even more than we do—to see that we have the things we need. Just trust Him. He'll provide. "Do not be anxious about anything, but in everything, by prayer and petition, with thanksgiving, present your requests to God. And the peace of God, which transcends all under-standing, will guard your hearts and your minds in Christ Jesus" (Philippians 4:6–7). We don't have to be anxious or worry; God will provide. We must simply trust Him to provide *today* what we need for today. It's a day-to-day trust that God is on our side.

How Does God Give?

Many of us may believe that God will provide, but we still worry about *how* He will provide. Sometimes, God may drop right into our laps the things we request and need. We pray and—wham!—it's there! What a testi-mony to the power and wonder of God! But God does not promise or guarantee that He will answer all our prayers in that manner. Many times as we pray for a need, God will give us the guidance and understanding of how to meet that need.

Let's say Chuck needs a job. Perhaps Chuck's got some extracurricular activities that cost money—he's dating, or there's a church trip he wants to go on. Whatever the reason, Chuck needs a job. So he prays, "Lord, I need a job." Quite a simple prayer, isn't it? Do you think, though, that the moment Chuck prays that prayer, the telephone's going to ring? "Hello, this is Mr. What-a-great-guy-to-have-for-a-boss calling. I have an opening at my restaurant and your name and number came to mind. So . . . would you like a job?"

It would be great if it worked that way, but God would probably prefer that Chuck act on his prayer and trust that He will provide him a job. As Chuck prays for a job, he steps out and begins seeking a job. He trusts that God will guide him to the places he should apply and that He will "open doors" to get him an interview and a job. Praying that God will *give* him a job can mean that Chuck prays that God will give him the direction he needs in finding a job.

A Matter of Moderation

"Give us today our daily bread" is a prayer of trust and dependence, looking to God to provide our physical needs *as we need them*—not before. Need money for a college education? Go ahead and talk to God about it, but don't expect scholarships or tuition money to drop into your lap while you're still in junior high. God provides what we need when we need it.

There's a great example of this in the Old Testament. When Moses led the children of Israel out of Egypt, God provided for their daily needs in the wilderness.

Then the LORD said to Moses, "I will rain down bread from heaven for you. The people are to go out each day and gather enough for that day. In this way I will test them and see whether they will follow my instructions. On the sixth day they are to prepare what they bring in, and that is to be twice as much as they gather on the other days."

That evening quail came and covered the camp, and in the morning there was a layer of dew around the camp. When the dew was gone, thin flakes like frost on the ground appeared on the desert floor. When the Israelites saw it, they said to each other,

"What is it?" For they did not know what it was.
Moses said to them, "It is the bread the LORD has
given you to eat.

This is what the LORD has commanded: 'Each
one is to gather as much as he needs. Take an omer
for each person you have in your tent.'"

The Israelites did as they were told; some gathered much, some little. And when they measured it
by the omer, he who gathered much did not have
too much, and he who gathered little did not have
too little. Each one gathered as much as he needed.

Then Moses said to them, "No one is to keep any
of it until morning."

However, some of them paid no attention to
Moses; they kept part of it until morning, but it was
full of maggots and began to smell. So Moses was
angry with them.

Exodus 16:4–5,13–20

God miraculously provided for the Israelites, but He
provided just what they needed. There was no point in
being greedy or worrying about what they'd need the
next day. The extra manna gathered out of greed or
worry only rotted. The command was to gather what was
needed; anything more showed a lack of trust in God.

He gives us what we need and what we can handle. He
gives us what we need to enjoy life and to enjoy Him.
"Give me neither poverty nor riches, but give me only
my daily bread. Otherwise, I may have too much and
disown you and say, 'Who is the LORD?' Or I may become
poor and steal, and so dishonor the name of my God"
(Proverbs 30:8–9).

God gives us what we need in just the right amount so that our trust will be in Him. People with an abundance of material things tend to trust their wealth rather than God. That's why Jesus said, "It is easier for a camel to go through the eye of a needle than for a rich man to enter the kingdom of God" (Matthew 19:24). Such a person's attitude is, "Why do I need God? I've already got everything I need. What else can God give me?" We shouldn't put our trust in ourselves or things; rather, we should trust the one who gives us those things.

> God gives us the things we need in just the right amount so that our trust will be in Him and not in material things.

Praying This Prayer for Others

"Give *us* today *our* daily bread." This is not a private prayer. God wants us to pray for other people's needs, too. You may have already noticed the group nature of this prayer: *Our* Father . . . *our* daily bread . . . *our* debts . . . *our* debtors . . . lead *us* not . . . . This is a prayer you pray for yourself . . . and others.

God also cares for our friends. It's a privilege to be a part of God's working in the life of another person by praying for that person. This is called *intercession.* In prayer, we are interceding for a friend; literally, we are praying in his or her place. Intercession is the idea of praying for someone else's need as if it were our own.

God can do great things when we pray for other people and their needs. There's an incredible sense of joy when we know we are part of God's work in someone else's life. Our intercession can change a life, bring someone closer to God, and meet some real needs. So, let's not make our prayers self-centered. Let's pray for others: family, friends, even people we've never met.

Conclusion

Don't be hesitant to ask God for things. Material things. Physical things. He will give us those things . . . at just the right time . . . in just the right amount. But while we are asking, let's remember the underlying requests that He be honored as King and His will would be done. He will always answer our requests and meet our needs, but we must be willing to let Him do it as He chooses. His way is always the best. So go ahead and ask!

▼

A C T S
—Responding to What I Read—

Adoration. Praise Him for being all-knowing; He not only knows what you need before you ask, He also knows the best way to meet that need. Then praise Him because He cares about you and desires to meet that need.

Confession. Oftentimes, we don't come to God with our needs. Instead, we attempt to meet those needs in our own power and in our own way. If you feel that you have done that, confess it to God and turn to depending on Him.

If you've asked things of God with selfish motives—just so that you could have those things for your own selfish pleasure—confess that to God and ask Him to make your wants in tune with His desires.

Thanksgiving. Think of the ways God has blessed you. Think of all the material things you have and thank God for each one. And as you bring to Him new requests and needs, thank Him—in advance!—for meeting them.

Supplication. Supplication is the heart of this chapter. So what needs do you have? What needs does your family have? Your friends? Those in leadership positions at school, national government, or the world?

I suggest you keep a prayer list of your needs and the needs of others you are praying for. If your list is lengthy, divide the requests up by days. Try something like this:

▼ **Sunday:** pray for your pastor and church services.

▼ **Monday:** pray for those in government.

▼ **Tuesday:** pray for needs of your family members.

▼ **Wednesday:** pray for your school.

▼ **Thursday:** pray for your friends.

▼ **Friday:** pray for your church youth group and the various ministries of your church.

▼ **Saturday:** pray for other churches in your area and mission work throughout the world.

Of course, the urgent needs you will want to pray for daily. By writing down your requests, you will remember to pray for all of them. Remember, The prayer of a righteous man is powerful and effective (James 5:16).

▼

EIGHT

Freedom!

Forgive us our debts,
as we also forgive our debtors.
Matthew 6:12

▼

This was a lot more boring than it looked on TV. At least that's what Colleen thought of the courtroom proceedings she was sitting through. She had witnessed an accident and was called to tell what she had seen. The injured driver was suing the man who had hit her, wanting the man to pay the medical bills. Colleen thought the man had caused injury and damage and he owed this woman something. In Colleen's eyes, it was the man's medical debts and he should pay them.

Colleen might have found the district court on the next floor more interesting. There a man had just been tried for several violent crimes: robbery, assault, and attemp-ted murder. The jury hadn't taken long to reach their verdict; it was obvious that this man was guilty. In pronouncing the man's sentence, the judge declared, "Sir, you have a history of breaking the law, hurting yourself and other people. No more. You're under obligation to pay for these crimes and I am going to see to it that you pay your debt to society." With that, the judge passed sentence.

▼

Debt. It's a word that makes me think of money: IOUs and credit card bills. Debt. It is something you owe to somebody else.

Debt can refer to more than just owing a few dollars. Think of this concept in legal terms. When someone is injured, the one who causes the injury owes the injured person compensation (a debt). When the law is broken, the transgressor (criminal, bad guy, man in the black hat) has to pay for what he's done. Until he pays (jail, restitution, community service, etc.), he owes a debt.

Debt is also a good word to explain our relationship to God. We've broken the law, too. God's laws. God created us with an ideal plan and purpose in mind, but through our sins we have gone against this ideal. We have wronged God. We owe a debt to God. (Although some Bible translations use the word *trespass* instead of *debt,* it's the same idea. We cross over into areas where God has placed a "No Trespassing" sign, and we wrong Him.)

How can we pay our debt to God? By serving time in jail? Being locked up in hell for eternity would not be my choice. Doing good to pay back what I've done? The Bible says that all our good works will never erase the debt we owe.

So how can we pay our debt to God?! That's just it; we can never pay that debt. But we can ask for His forgiveness. We can ask God to cancel the debt. That's what this next prayer request is all about: "Forgive us our debts." The good news is that this prayer is a prayer that God always answers.

The Basis for Forgiveness: God's Character

One of my favorite people in the Old Testament is David. There are a lot of wonderful stories about David in the Books of 1 and 2 Samuel. But there's one story out of David's life that is not so pleasant. It was a time later in his life when he sinned . . . big time.

First, he was looking where he shouldn't have been looking. He lusted and coveted after Bathsheba, another man's wife. Then he committed adultery with her. When Bathsheba became pregnant, he was deceitful. Finally, to cover up his actions, he had her husband, Uriah, killed. David was loaded down with sin and guilt.

It was a pretty serious situation, but it didn't end there. David looked to God and asked for forgiveness. "Have mercy on me, O God, according to your unfailing love; according to your great compassion blot out my transgressions" (Psalm 51:1). God didn't have to forgive David, but he did. Why? Because it is a part of God's character to forgive.

When David prayed this, he asked for God's mercy and forgiveness based on two things: God's unfailing love and His compassion. God's love for David didn't cease when David sinned. He wanted to forgive David much more than David wanted to be forgiven.

It's the same for you and me. God's compassion is so immense that He doesn't want to see us in slavery to sin or burdened down with guilt. His love compels Him to free us. As our perfect Father, He does not scold us when we fall, but rather He is ready and waiting to sweep us into His arms and love us. We don't have to be afraid of Him. He wants to free us and restore us even more that we desire to be freed and restored. "But you are a forgiving God, gracious and compassionate, slow to anger and abounding in love. Therefore you did not desert them" (Nehemiah 9:17).

What Do I Have to Do to Be Forgiven?

Even though God is full of love and compassion, He will not just sweep our sins under the rug. Our sins have to be paid for. That's why Jesus calls our sins *debts*. A debt has to be paid. The problem is that you and I are incapable of ever paying off that debt. The debt of our sins has destined us to spend eternity in hell.

There is a solution, though: Jesus Christ. Perhaps you are familiar with the song "He Paid a Debt":

He paid a debt he did not owe,
I owed a debt I could not pay;
I needed someone to wash my sins away.
And now I sing a brand new song,
Amazing grace, all day long;
Christ Jesus paid the debt that I could never pay.

We can be free because Jesus Christ has paid the price for our sins. Our debt has been paid!

But this gift of forgiveness, is only ours if we accept it. To receive it we must admit that we are sinners and that we are sorry for our sins. It's one thing to admit our sins; it's another thing to be sorry for our sins.

You've seen those old courtroom dramas. The accused person is on the witness stand and, as the pressure from the prosecuting attorney builds, the accused shouts, "Yes, I did it! And I'm glad I did it!" He then lets go with a melodramatic sinister laugh.

The man has confessed to the crime, but that doesn't mean that he is sorry for what he did; he is only admitting that he did it.

The Bible's definition of confession goes much further than just admitting sins. Real confession is seeing sin as God sees it. How does God see sin? He hates it. He so despises sin that He will have nothing to do with it. When we see sin as God sees it, we, too, hate it and desire to have nothing to do with it anymore.

To become a Christian, we first admit our sinfulness and ask Jesus to forgive us of all our sins and make us new. But what about the sins we commit *after* we become Christians? We still need to confess them. Our debt was completely paid when Christ died on the cross, but we still must lay our new sins at the foot of the cross.

▼

Let's think about Leroy for a moment. One day, Leroy decided to borrow the family car. Bad move, Leroy. You see, Leroy's father had told him never to use the car without permission or without telling them where he was going. Leroy could not take the car out of town until his dad thought he was a more experienced driver.

But on this particular occasion, Leroy's parents were gone for the evening. But the car was there. Leroy really wanted to go with his friends to the basketball game fifty miles away. So what did Leroy do? That's right, he took the car. He knew his parents wouldn't return until late, and Leroy figured he and his friends could travel the fifty miles, attend the game, and be back before Mom and Dad came home.

And it worked. Leroy got back without his parents ever knowing . . . or so he thought. Leroy forgot to refill the gas tank. Leroy's dad got in the car the next morning and noticed his once-full gas tank was now almost empty. It didn't take Leroy's dad long to figure out what had happened. But Leroy's father never mentioned the offense. He waited to see if Leroy would step forward with the truth.

Meanwhile, Leroy's conscience was getting the best of him. He found it hard to look his dad in the eye so he avoided him. Leroy had wanted to go fishing with his dad the next weekend—something they had always enjoyed together—but Leroy felt too bad about what he had done to ask to go fishing.

Was Leroy still his father's son? Of course he was, *but there was a barrier in their relationship.* Leroy was always a son, but until he talked to his dad about what he had done he would not be free to enjoy the full benefits of that relationship.

That's how it is with our heavenly Father. As Christians, we are His children, and nothing can change that. But unconfessed sin can keep us from enjoying the full benefits of a child of God. Unconfessed sin is a barrier in our fellowship with our Father. "He who conceals his sins does not prosper, but whoever confesses and renounces them finds mercy" (Proverbs 28:13). We are still Christians, but we won't prosper until we pray, "Forgive us our debts."

Let's Get Specific

When we pray, "Forgive us our debts," we need to get specific about what those debts are. If we sin, we must admit to God *how* we sinned.

We often pray vaguely: "God, if I've sinned, forgive me." But we need to put some thought behind our prayers. Have I sinned against God? Is there something I've done—or not done—that I need to confess? I don't dwell on this to feel bad about myself, but I want to confess anything and everything that will keep me from enjoying God and the full life He offers.

Do you know when the best time to confess sin is? The moment we realize we have sinned. Why put it off until bedtime prayers? We need to confess the wrong, get it behind us, and get on with enjoying life.

"But what if there's some sin I don't know about? Won't my unknown sins keep me from walking with God?" Don't worry. We can't confess something we don't know about. The only time we need to confess is when we do sin. The problem arises only when we know of a particular sin but don't confess it.

One night when I was in high school, I was driving through Houston with my girlfriend. I noticed my dad's van was about to run out of gas, so I pulled into the first gas station I saw. I opened my wallet and quickly realized that I didn't have enough money to buy gas to get us home. I had a major problem. But at that same moment another van pulled into the gas station and out stepped the youth minister of the church I had been attending.

I approached him and explained my predicament. "Jack," I asked, "All I need is a couple of dollars. I can pay you back the next time I see you."

Being the nice guy that he was, he willingly loaned me the two dollars.

Eleven years later, that incident came to mind. Why I remembered it, I don't know. I hadn't thought about it in eleven years, but I remembered it now, and I remembered that I had never paid him back those two dollars. Boy, did I feel bad. I tried to dismiss it. After all, the incident was so long ago. It was just two dollars. But God wouldn't let me forget it, however trivial it now seemed.

I had to make a few phone calls, but I finally tracked down Jack's address. He was now a missionary in Mexico. I wrote Jack an apologetic letter and stuck several dollars in the envelope (I figured with eleven years of inflation, those two dollars were worth a lot more now).

For eleven years I had carried a debt and failed to keep a promise. Yet during those eleven years, God did some incredible things in my life.

God blessed me in spite of the fact that I carried around this debt to Jack. Granted, it was an honest mistake. I just plain forgot. It only became an issue in my ministry and walk with God when the Holy Spirit reminded me of my debt and convicted me of my need to correct the matter.

> *If we are unwilling to forgive others, our ability to receive God's forgiveness is limited.*

We don't have to make up sins to confess. It's the work of the Holy Spirit to show us our sins and lead us to confession. We don't have to convict ourselves. But we must deal with the sins we do know of in our lives.

Forgiving Others

The first condition to receiving forgiveness is that we must confess our sin to God. The second condition to receiving God's forgiveness is that we must be willing to forgive others. Notice that this request has two parts: "Forgive us our debts, as we also have forgiven our debtors." This is the only part of the Model Prayer on which Jesus offered any further explanation. At the close of the Model Prayer, he referred to this request: "For if you forgive men when they sin against you, your heavenly Father will also forgive you. But if you do not forgive men their sins, your Father will not forgive your sins" (Matthew 6:14–15).

Is God's ability to forgive limited? No, but if we are unwilling to forgive others, our ability to receive God's forgiveness is limited. God can have nothing to do with those things that are opposite to His character. A holy God cannot associate Himself with unholiness. A God whose nature is to forgive, cannot pass on forgiveness to a heart where forgiveness is not already present.

"But you don't know what she did to me! I can never forgive her for that!" Fine, just don't expect God to forgive you. How does that wrong thing she did against you compare to all the wrong things you've done against God? Jesus brought this truth home in a great story:

> Therefore, the kingdom of heaven is like a king who wanted to settle accounts with his servants. As he began the settlement, a man who owed him ten thousand talents was brought to him. Since he was not able to pay, the master ordered that he and his wife and his children and all that he had be sold to repay the debt.
>
> The servant fell on his knees before him. "Be patient with me," he begged, "and I will pay back everything." The servant's master took pity on him, canceled the debt and let him go.
>
> But when that servant went out, he found one of his fellow servants who owed him a hundred de-

narii. He grabbed him and began to choke him. "Pay back what you owe me!" he demanded.

His fellow servant fell to his knees and begged him, "Be patient with me, and I will pay you back."

But he refused. Instead, he went off and had the man thrown into prison until he could pay the debt. When the other servants saw what had happened, they were greatly distressed and went and told their master everything that had happened.

Then the master called the servant in. "You wicked servant," he said, "I canceled all that debt of yours because you begged me to. Shouldn't you have had mercy on your fellow servant just as I had on you?" In anger his master turned him over to the jailers to be tortured, until he should pay back all he owed.

This is how my heavenly Father will treat each of you unless you forgive your brother from your heart.

Matthew 18:23–35

The man had a large debt canceled, but he was unwilling to forgive a small debt! Jesus used exaggeration to make a point: the ones who are forgiven great debts ought to forgive others of minor debts. The things other people have done against us are insignificant compared to the things we've done against God.

In Psalm 66:18 we read "If I had cherished sin in my heart, the Lord would not have listened." This verse does not just refer to cherishing (holding onto) our own sins, but cherishing the sins of others. In other words, I won't let the matter rest. I cherish what they did to me in the sense that, every time I see the persons, I think about the wrongs they did. I'm holding on to their mistakes and won't let go.

Steve and Karla represent two young people I know. They developed a good, close relationship. But after dating over six months, they sinned sexually. They were both Christians and immediately felt the conviction of God for what they had done. Although they acknowledged their sin, their relationship deteriorated. Things never got better between them, so after a few more months, they went their separate ways.

Steve recovered from the bad experience and moved on. Karla, however, would not let go. She blamed Steve for the sin they both committed, and she told me that she could not forgive him for what he had done to her. Karla's attitude toward Steve was eating away at her. Karla's inability to forgive affected her ability to worship at church and it ruined her friendship with people who were also friends with Steve. Her relationship with God deteriorated. Karla ended up in counseling because of her unwillingness to forgive.

You've heard the phrase, "Forgive and forget." It may be impossible actually to forget, but we can forgive and quit bringing up the matter. Forgiveness literally means *to hurl away.* If God can hurl our sins away—as great as they are—then we can certainly do the same with others' wrongs against us.

> Then Peter came to Jesus and asked, "Lord, how many times shall I forgive my brother when he sins against me? Up to seven times?"
>
> Jesus answered, "I tell you, not seven times, but seventy-seven times."
> Matthew 18:21–22

How many times has God forgiven you and me . . . for the same sin? We should do it for others.

The Freedom of Forgiveness

There's a freedom in forgiveness when we let go of the mistakes of others and when we give our own sins into the hands of God so that He can hurl them into the depths of the sea. (Micah 7:19) That freedom of forgiveness comes when we confess, repent, and forgive others.

Forgiveness frees us from the debt we owe God. One of the best feelings I've had is making a final car payment. No more debt! It is *great* to get out from under a financial burden and have some extra money for awhile.

That feeling of freedom is even greater when I think about the debt God has removed. I'm free to live in a right relationship with God and enjoy all the benefits of that relationship: loved, secure, full of joy, full of hope, and with a sense of direction and fulfillment.

There is freedom that comes when I forgive others, too. I am freed from bitterness, anger, and hatred. When we are full of anger and bitterness toward someone else, does it effect them? Not very much. But it eats away at us! When we forgive, bitterness is replaced by joy. Unforgiveness is replaced by love.

When we forgive and are forgiven, we are free to love. We become emotionally stronger . . . and blessed! "Blessed is he whose transgressions are forgiven, whose sins are covered. Blessed is the man whose sin the lord does not count against him and in whose spirit is no deceit" (Psalm 32:1–2).

▼

A C T S
—Responding to What I Read—

Adoration. Praise God because He is full of mercy. Praise Him for His unfailing love. Praise Him for His compassion.

Confession. Confession is the heart of this chapter. Are there things in your life that you have swept under the rug? Talk to God about your sins. Be specific. As He reveals sins in your life, confess them. Remember: He is full of compassion and wants to forgive you and free you.

Thanksgiving. Thank Jesus for dying on the cross to remove your sins. Thank Him for forgiving you so many times, even though your sins caused Him such pain on the cross. Thank Him for always listening and always forgiving.

Supplication. Do you have friends who are struggling with sin? Do you have friends who are refusing to acknowledge there is sin in their lives? Pray for them, asking God to convict them and open their eyes to the freedom and forgiveness of God.

Do you have somebody that you need to forgive? Forgive him now. If it's difficult, ask for God's strength in overcoming an unforgiving attitude. Ask Him to give you the ability to forgive even as He has forgiven you. Then, if necessary, go to that person and express your forgiveness. By humbling yourself and going to that person with forgiveness, you may open the door for a restored relationship. Jesus did it for you, so do it for somebody else.

▼

N I N E

Avoiding the Pitfalls

And lead us not into temptation,
but deliver us from the evil one.
Matthew 6:13

▼

Looking back, Darrell wished there had been a large, yellow, blinking sign.

Darrell flew to Portland to spend the first week of August with his dad's family. He and his cousin Josh had such a good time together at the Memorial Day family reunion that both sets of parents agreed to let Darrell spend the week in Portland with Josh. Darrell was elated.

Things were going well, too. Darrell enjoyed his Uncle Dave and Aunt Martha even though he had rarely seen them and hardly knew them. He and Josh certainly seemed to hit it off, too. But when Josh wanted to take Darrell out to meet his friends, things changed.

"Let me show you how we do things here in Portland," Josh said to Darrell as he popped a cassette in the tape deck and turned the volume up in his little Sunbird. "There's a party we don't want to miss. Don't worry about not knowing anybody. I'll introduce you around and I'll bet you'll get lucky before the night's over."

"Lucky?"

"Yeah, lots of females there," said Josh, oblivious to Darrell's small town naiveté. "But first," Josh continued, looking and reaching into the back seat without slowing the Pontiac down. He pulled a plastic grocery bag into the front seat. "Get us started, Darrell."

Darrell reached into the bag, felt the cold aluminum tops of a six-pack and judged from Josh's changed attitude that these were probably not Coca-Colas. He was right. He pulled from the bag a six-pack of Coors.

What have I gotten into? Darrel thought.

Darrell was torn inside. Part of this fifteen-year-old from a small town was drawn to the adventure of it all. It sounded dangerously exciting. He admitted that these temptations were . . . tempting.

Darrell also knew he would be a fool to do it. He was a Christian; he knew there was a better life than this. He didn't need this. He didn't want it. But still . . .

"What're you waiting for? Open one of those cans and let's get started," Josh said. Darrell just sat there staring at the top of the six-pack. The war inside him drowned out the sounds of the heavy metal music in his ears.

▼

Temptations are all around us. The trick is knowing how to avoid them. That's why Jesus gave us this last request: "Lead us not into temptation but deliver us from evil." It seems only natural that, after confessing our past sins, we seek God's help in avoiding any future sins.

Would You Tempt Me, God?

No, God will not tempt us to sin. He hates sin, but loves us. God will not lead someone He loves into something

He hates. "When tempted, no one should say, 'God is tempting me.' For God cannot be tempted by evil, nor does he tempt anyone" (James 1:13).

"If God will not tempt me, then why am I praying this request? Why am I praying about something that God has already said He wouldn't do?"

That's a fair question, but look again at what the request is saying . . . and what it is *not* saying. We are not praying, "Don't tempt me," but "*Lead* us *not* into temptation." We can ask God to help us not fall into temptation. This is a prayer for protection and strength in the midst of the temptations already around us.

Being tempted is not a sin. After all, Jesus was tempted. The issue is what you and I do with those temptations. Temptation is not the sin, but it can lead to sin. "But each one is tempted when, by his own evil desire, he is dragged away and enticed. Then, after desire has conceived, it gives birth to sin; and sin, when it is fullgrown, gives birth to death" (James 1:14–15). Temptation works on our desires. When we allow our minds to dwell on the temptation, our unchecked desires give birth to sin.

The Devil Made Me Do It?

"If God doesn't tempt me, then who does?" That leads us to only one other source, the one who wants to see us stumble and fall: Satan. But Satan does not make us sin. The old excuse, "The devil made me do it" just doesn't cut it. He will do everything in his power to entice us, but he can't force us into sin. It's still our choice.

Although Satan can't take away a Christian's relationship with God, he will try to weaken that relationship. As long as we live in sin, there is a barrier in our relationship with God, and our witness and walk are compromised. A weak, backslidden Christian is no threat to Satan. Therefore, he will do whatever he can to keep us in sin.

At the beginning of His ministry, Jesus was tempted by Satan. These weren't just casual temptations. Satan gave it everything he had. After all, who was more of a threat to Satan's demonic kingdom than Jesus? Who walked more with the heavenly Father than Jesus? You can be sure that Satan gave it his best shot.

Satan didn't give up, either. "When the devil had finished all this tempting, he left him until an opportune time" (Luke 4:13). Satan was determined to pull Jesus down, so he came back again and again and again.

He does the same with us, too. Just because we resist Satan once and gain a victory over sin doesn't mean Satan's not going to try again. He will. But we must do the things that Jesus did to avoid the pitfalls of temptation: He walked closely with His heavenly Father, and He knew His enemy.

Ways We Are Tempted

The best ploy Satan uses is to tempt us in our weaknesses. Is there a particular sin or habit that you easily fall into? If so, that's the first place he'll start. I have never been tempted to rob a convenience store. I've got pretty strong feelings against armed robbery, so Satan would be wasting his time trying to tempt me in this way.

There are other areas of my life, though, that are not strong. There are some sins that are "fun" (even though that fun may last only for a moment), and it's easy for

Satan to entice me with these sins. We all have our own particular weak areas where Satan tempts us. Some people are easily enticed to follow the crowd, to drink, to abuse drugs, to be promiscuous, or to indulge in pornographic materials. Other sins are not so obvious, but people still fall easily into them: gossip, impure thoughts, maliciously cutting others down.

What are your weak areas? Those are the very areas to guard, for that is where Satan will first strike. We should never put ourselves in situations where we know we are vulnerable to temptation and sin. It's one thing to resolve not to go drinking this weekend, it's another thing to avoid the parties and situations where alcohol will be present. It's one thing to say we do not want to lust or have impure thoughts, it's another thing to stay away from the movies and magazines that lead us to lust.

> *"I can't keep the birds from flying over my head, but I can keep them from building a nest in my hair."*

Martin Luther said, "I can't keep the birds from flying over my head, but I can keep them from building a nest in my hair." Let's not give the devil an opportunity to tempt our weaknesses.

Don't ever let your guard down. It doesn't matter how strong a Christian we become, we still need to guard against those weak areas in our lives. Chris is a prime example. Chris went to youth camp and had an incredible encounter with God. He made a recommitment to Christ and openly dealt with some sins in his life. Chris began growing in his Christian walk. But Chris fell hard. Why? He let down his guard. Satan lured Chris into thinking that, since the battle was over, he could return to the old places where the temptation was so strong.

Have you ever known anybody like that? The Christian may rationalize, "God has given me victory over sexual sin. I can go out with my girlfriend and not worry about sexual temptation. Instead, we'll just sit alone in the car and read the Bible and pray." Watch out! This Christian has let his guard down and allowed Satan to maneuver him back into a weak, vulnerable position.

Don't ever let down your guard. On the night Jesus was arrested, Peter boasted of his strong stand for Jesus. Jesus knew better. He told Peter that he would deny Him three times that very night. In the garden, when Jesus was praying, he challenged Peter to pray also. "Watch and pray so that you will not fall into temptation. The spirit is willing, but the body is weak" (Matthew 26:41). Peter didn't watch, he didn't pray; instead he let down his guard. The result: he denied Jesus.

Peter learned his lesson well: Keep your guard up. Never overestimate your own strength. And never underestimate your enemy's strength. Years later, Peter wrote, "Be self-controlled and alert. Your enemy the devil prowls around like a roaring lion looking for someone to devour" (1 Peter 5:8).

There's one other way Satan works. Sometimes Satan will tempt us with good things. . . .

"Good things?! What's wrong with good things?"

There's nothing inherently wrong with good things, but sometimes Satan will tempt us with good things in order to keep us from *the best things.*

Let's say there's a good movie coming on TV . . . or a championship game that you've been wanting to see. There's nothing wrong with the movie or with the sporting event. So you sit down and lose two hours in front of the television when you should have been catching up on your English assignment.

What if you told your father you'd have the yard mowed before he came home. Or you were going to call that friend and apologize and patch up your relationship. But instead, you watched TV. Consequently, your English grade gets worse, you face a potentially explosive situation with your dad, or your relationship with that friend deteriorates further. Yes, the game or the movie may have been a good thing, but you let it rob you of a better thing.

Second Corinthians 11:14 warns us that "Satan himself masquerades as an angel of light." If he can't get to us with "bad" things, he'll try to get at us with "good" things. That's the point of this request, "Lead us not into temptation, but deliver us from the evil one."

▼ God, lead me to be aware of when I am being tempted. Help me to recognize those unrecognized temptations.

▼ God, help me to realize when I am walking into a situation where I might be vulnerable and liable to fall into sin.

▼ God, give me strength to resist the temptations I face.

▼ God, help me to discern the devil's scheming. Lead me away from accepting the "good" Satan is tempting me with. Lead me away from the "good" that will keep me from doing what You really want me to do.

That's the heart of this request. We're not asking God to keep evil away from us, we're asking God to keep us from falling into evil.

Finding the Way Out of Temptation

How, then, does God deliver us from evil? God does not save us, then leave us to fight sin and temptation on our own. Just as we cannot save ourselves, God does not expect us to live the Christian life ourselves. He's there for us. I find even more encouragement in knowing that Jesus understands and sympathizes. He's been there.

> For we do not have a high priest who is unable to sympathize with our weaknesses, but we have one who has been tempted in every way, just as we are yet was without sin.
> Hebrews 4:15

> Because he himself suffered when he was tempted, he is able to help those who are being tempted.
> Hebrews 2:18

Jesus well knows the struggle with temptation. You and I cannot appreciate the degree or intensity of temptation that Jesus went through. I'm sure Satan worked at tempting the Son of God far harder than he's ever worked at tempting you or me.

Jesus has been there and He's here for us. The key is for you and me to stay close to Jesus. He was able to overcome temptation, and He is able to help us overcome temptation. We must stay close to Him.

God does not expect us to live the Christian life ourselves. He's there for us.

If we sin, it's because we let our guard down and take our eyes off Jesus. "I couldn't help it. I couldn't resist this one temptation," is not a valid excuse. God so cares about us that, if there were a temptation that could so irresisably overwhelm us, He wouldn't even let such a powerful influence near us. "No temptation has seized you except what is common to man. And God is faithful; he will not let you be tempted beyond what you can bear. But when you are tempted, he will also provide a way out so that you can stand up under it" (1 Corinthians 10:13).

God is there to deliver! No sin or temptation comes near us that God does not also give us the strength to overcome. If we really couldn't help but fall into a particular sin, then God wouldn't allow that temptation to get near us in the first place.

So if you are tempted, God has also given you the power and resources not to sin. God always provides a way out. What is that way? Lean on Jesus, have the desire to do what is right, and He'll make it clear what that way out is.

Where did Jesus find His "way out?" The three temptations of Jesus that are recorded in the New Testament have one common element. Jesus' "way out" was always through Scripture. He didn't try to rationalize His way out of temptation. He didn't make excuses. He just quoted Scripture. That's a good principle for us, too. Know God's Word. Then when those times of temptation come, God can call to our minds His Word and give us the strength to walk away untouched. "I have hidden your word in my heart that I might not sin against you" (Psalm 119:11).

Do you find yourself easily giving in to a particular sin? Find some Bible verses that relate to that sin and commit them to heart. Memorize them. Then when that temptation rears its head again, you can come against it with the Word of God. If you need help in finding appropriate verses, use a Bible concordance or a topical

Bible. You can also ask your pastor, youth minister, or friend to help you locate some key verses to memorize.

Keep Your Eyes on Jesus

Billy Beacham tells how they train dogs at one particular guard school. These dogs are put through extensive training in order to work as guard dogs for large estates. When the school feels a dog has been sufficiently trained, the dog is put through one final test.

The dog is first starved for several days. Then the dog is brought into a room and given the command to sit and stay. A few moments later, they bring in a large, juicy steak and put it right under the nose of the potential guard dog. The dog passes the test based on its decision at that moment. Will the dog obey the command to sit and stay or will the dog give in to its own ravenous hunger and devour the steak?

Of course, the dog that goes for the steak fails the test. A dog that succumbs to the steak might later succumb if a burglar or intruder distracted him with a steak.

The dogs who passed the test were the dogs who kept their eyes fixed on their master. The smell of the cooked meat enticed their noses, their mouths were watering, but they kept their eyes fixed on the one who gave them the command.

Do you see the point? We so often get in trouble because we begin to look at the temptation we are being offered. The more we look at that temptation, the more the desire grows within us to give in. But, just like guard dogs, we must keep our eyes on our Master.

▼

A C T S
—Responding to What I Read—

Adoration. Praise God for His faithfulness. He is always there to provide a way out so that you can stand up even under temptation. Praise Him for His love that leads Him to provide that way out.

Confession. Do you find yourself giving in to certain temptations too easily? Confess to God, then, those times you have not looked to Him for deliverance. If you've made excuses for your sins, admit that to Him, too, and express your desire not to give in to temptations.

Thanksgiving. Thank Jesus for His understanding of what you are going through. Thank Him for His sympathetic nature, for knowing the struggle you face with temptation. Thank Him for His presence to encourage You and strengthen you.

Supplication. Ask God to give you discernment—to be able to know right from wrong, to be able to distinguish between what Satan offers and the best God desires. Ask God to keep you strong in the face of temptations and make you aware of the way out that He has provided.

If there is a particular habit you are struggling with, ask God to give you direction from His Word in overcoming that habit. Ask Him to give you appropriate verses to memorize. "Let not my heart be drawn to what is evil, to take part in wicked deeds with men who are evildoers; let me not eat of their delicacies" (Psalm 141:4).

▼

T E N

Let Me Hear An "Amen!"

For yours is the kingdom and the power
and the glory forever. Amen.

Matthew 6:13

▼

The Model Prayer takes us full circle. We are ending where we started. We began by seeking God's honor in our prayers and lives. We then sought His kingdom and the display of His kingdom in our lives. Then we sought to have His will accomplished. We sought His will concerning our physical needs, relational needs, and spiritual needs.

Believing God can do all that, we come right back to seeing Him honored in all these things. "God, I believe You and praise You because You can do all things. After all, 'Yours is the kingdom and the power and the glory forever.' The kingdom is Yours ["your kingdom come"], the power is Yours ["your will be done"], and the glory is Yours ["hallowed be your name"]. I praise You because within Your kingdom You have the will and the power to accomplish these things, and You will accomplish them in a way that will honor and glorify You."

We close our prayer in praise—praise of who He is and what He will accomplish. It's a way of thanking God *in advance* for what He's going to do. "Surely the arm of the Lord is not too short to save, nor his ear too dull to hear" (Isaiah 59:1). We end up in praise to God because He has heard us. We end up in praise to God because His arm is not too short—He has complete power to meet our requests and needs. So we praise Him, thanking Him for what He is doing and for what He is going to do.

Praise—the Right Thing to Do

It is good to praise God because it is right. It is what God alone deserves, and it is what we owe Him in light of all that He has done for us.

Have you ever heard of the *Lady Elgin*? The *Lady Elgin* was a passenger ship. Or at least it was until it was in a tragic accident on Lake Michigan. Right off the Chicago port, the *Lady Elgin* was sinking with over three hundred passengers on board.

Of the people on the shoreline witnessing this tragedy, two were seminary students. One of them was a well-trained swimmer, so he dove into the ice-cold water and swam out to the sinking ship. He snatched one of the drowning victims and swam to the shore. He deposited the person on the beach and, to everyone's amazement, he swam back to the ship! He made this trip twenty-three times and rescued twenty-three people. Unfortunately, the remaining three hundred passengers drowned.

This heroic act took its toll on the brave rescuer. Making that trip twenty-three times in the frigid cold water was so much of a strain on the body of this young swimmer that he became ill. Severely ill. This hero lived the rest of his life as an invalid.

We applaud such heroism, but the sad part of his story is that, of the twenty-three people whose lives were saved by this incredible man, not one ever thanked him. He sacrificed his health for their sakes, but not one of them ever visited him or even wrote him a note of thanks.

This brave swimmer did not perform his life-threatening heroics in order to be thanked. But twenty-three people owed him their lifelong gratitude. The swimmer didn't ask for thanks, but he certainly deserved it.

We owe God our unending thanks and praise. When we think about the sacrifice that Jesus made to save us, we are drawn to thank Him. When we think about all that He offers us, we are moved to thankfulness.

"It is good to praise the Lord and make music to your name, O Most High" (Psalm 92:1).

Praise Is Pleasant

Another reason we should praise God is because of what it does for us: praising God makes us feel good! "Praise the Lord. How good it is to sing praises to our God, how pleasant and fitting to praise him!" (Psalm 147:1). When we praise God, God gets the honor and glory that He deserves, but He gives us the joy! We just can't outgive God. We give Him praise and in return He gives us joy!

> We give him praise and in return He gives us joy!

Praise is a way of getting life into perspective. Life sometimes gets out of hand because we're focusing on the problems around us. Stress sets in when those problems seem bigger than our ability to handle them. Our perspective on life becomes distorted.

When we praise God, a balance returns to life. Praise is centered on God. Circumstances may throw some wild curves at us, but when we praise God, we see Him for all that He is and all that He is doing in our lives. We praise Him for His care, His faithfulness, His power over life and problems, and His love and His willingness to befriend us. When we praise God, we begin to see Him in all His power and majesty, and suddenly the problems in life don't seem so overwhelming.

Praise will cause us to focus on the answer to our problems: Jesus Christ.

In this world you will have trouble. But take heart! I have overcome the world.
John 16:33

The one who is in you is greater than the one who is in the world.
1 John 4:4

Praising God will not make our problems go away, but praise will cause us to focus on the answer to our problems: Jesus Christ. Praising Him helps us concentrate on the One who is bigger than any problem. From the perspective of Jesus Christ, we can have joy even in the midst of problems.

How to Praise God

Try the ABCs of praise. Go through the alphabet and think of the things for which you can praise Him. "I praise You because you are so **A**wesome. I praise You because you are **B**igger than my problems. I praise You because You are **C**aring. I praise You because You are **D**ivine. I praise You because . . .

Read the Psalms aloud. The Psalms were the Old
Testament hymn book. Originally, these Psalms were
songs sung to God. Be creative and make up your own
melodies to sing these Psalms to God. If singing is not
your thing, you can at least read them aloud. Try reading
Psalm 96 aloud.

Sing to the LORD a new song;
   sing to the LORD, all the earth.
Sing to the LORD, praise his name;
   proclaim his salvation day after day.
Declare his glory among the nations,
   his marvelous deeds among all peoples.

For great is the LORD and most worthy of praise;
   he is to be feared above all gods.
For all the gods of the nations are idols,
   but the LORD made the heavens.
Splendor and majesty are before him;
   strength and glory are in his sanctuary.

Ascribe to the LORD, O families of nations,
   ascribe to the LORD glory and strength.
Ascribe to the LORD the glory due his name;
   bring an offering and come into his courts.
Worship the LORD in the splendor of his holiness;
   tremble before him, all the earth.
Say among the nations, "The LORD reigns."
   The world is firmly established, it cannot be moved;
   he will judge the peoples with equity.
Let the heavens rejoice, let the earth be glad;
   let the sea resound, and all that is in it;
   let the fields be jubilant, and everything in them.

Then all the trees of the forest will sing for joy;
　　they will sing before the LORD, for he comes,
　　he comes to judge the earth.
He will judge the world in righteousness
　　and the peoples in his truth.

There are a lot of other Psalms that can easily draw you into praise. For starters, you might try Psalms 19, 24, 29, 33, 47, 65, 66, 93, 98, 104, 111, 139, and 148.

You may also know some great songs or choruses that praise God. And don't forget the old hymns. Yes, hymns. Some of these hymns we have sung so much that we can sing them without thinking. But try some of these old hymns again while thinking about the words. Don't sing the words, just speak them.

Read the words of this great old hymn:

O Worship the King
O worship the King, all glorious above,
And gratefully sing His wonderful love;
Our Shield and Defender, the Ancient of Days,
Pavilioned in splendor, and girded with praise.
Frail children of dust, and feeble as frail,
In Thee do we trust, nor find Thee to fail:
Thy mercies how tender, how firm to the end,
Our Maker, Defender, Redeemer, and Friend.

The best way for us to praise God, though, is to let it come naturally. As we pray, we are concentrating on a loving Father who hears and answers our every need. The closer we get to God in prayer, the more we will be drawn to praise Him. And more praise will just naturally flow from our hearts.

▼

A   C   T   S
—Responding to What I Read—

Adoration. Adoration is, of course, the heart of this chapter. Use some of the above suggestions and begin forming the habit of praise.

Confession. If you have taken God's kingdom, power and glory for granted, confess that to Him. If necessary, confess the sin of ingratitude. If you have coasted through the worship services of your church, confess that to God, and commit to Him that you will make a conscious effort to praise Him in the worship services and in your private times with Him.

Thanksgiving. Thanksgiving is the companion to praise. Praise is directed to who God *is*. Thanksgiving is directed to what God *has done*. Following the suggestions above, thank God for the various ways He has shown Himself to you and worked in your life.

Supplication. Ask God to make you aware of the many ways He is working in your life. Ask Him to make you sensitive to His presence and work in your life so that you can avoid the sin of ingratitude.

▼

Where Do I Go from Here?

▼

Owen was a bookworm. He even fit the stereotype. Glasses that were usually held together with masking tape. A pocket protector crammed with leaky pens. Pants two inches above his white socks. Some would call him the classic nerd. He was always reading. Although Owen had a preference for science and science fiction, he read all sorts of books. Regardless of the subject, Owen's preferred method of learning was with a book.

That is why Owen never took driver's ed. He just read about driving. He read the state handbooks and defensive driving pamphlets. He studied traffic laws. On his eighteenth birthday, Owen knew he was ready to take his driving test. It didn't matter that he had never been behind the wheel of his mother's car. He had read all there was to read. He knew the basics. What more was there?

Owen failed miserably. A 100 on the written exam (of course), but a 47 on the driving exam. Owen learned that the only way to learn to drive is . . . to drive.

▼

Now that you know the basics of prayer shown in the Model Prayer, what's next? That's simple: you pray!

It's just like Owen and his driving test. The only way anyone is going to learn to drive is to get behind the wheel of a car and practice driving.

You've read about prayer. But knowing about prayer does not make you a pray-er. You've got to get in there and pray! Talking to God may be new to you or you may feel a little uncomfortable with it, but just jump in. Praying will become easier and more comfortable as you do it. But nothing will make you a better pray-er than praying will!

> Nothing will make you a better pray-er than praying will!

Making Prayer a Part of Your Day

Set Aside a Time for Prayer

Talking to God is something we can do anytime and anywhere. Yet, because prayer is so easy to begin, it is easy for us to forget to begin! We must make time for prayer.

Is there a time that's better than others? I prefer the mornings. Before I face the day, I talk to God about the day I am about to face. My praying focuses in on who God is and gets my life and the day's events in proper perspective. Of course, the mornings are not the only times you can spend alone with God, but it's a great way to begin a day.

The important thing, though, is to spend time with God in prayer. Make a special time for prayer and guard that time. Make an agreement with yourself that you will not watch TV . . . or talk on the telephone . . . or go to sleep until you've spent time alone with God.

Let God Talk to You

Think of prayer as a conversation with your heavenly Father. And just like any good conversation, it involves two people talking to each other. As you daily meet with God in prayer, allow some time for reading the Bible. Ask God to speak to you through what you read. You don't have to read big chunks of Scripture every day, just a chapter or a passage. Then pray about what you read.

If you read a command or see an example of how to live, talk to God and ask Him to guide you in following that command or example. Many times God will show us sins in our lives through His Word. Confess to God the sins He reveals.

Reading the Bible and praying go hand in hand. You talk to God; God talks to you. It's a safe assumption (based on my own experience) that if you don't take time to read God's Word, you'll soon quit taking time to pray. So, as with your prayer life, plan to spend time daily in God's Word. Set a time and place and stick with it!

Just Do It!

What is the greatest thing we could do? Be a world-renown preacher who speaks to thousands and thousands of people? Be the next Mother Theresa? Be a great statesman-politician who helps nations cooperate and find peace? These things are important and good, but the greatest thing we can do is to stand in prayer before the God and Creator of the entire universe and talk with Him. What greater honor could we give our friends than to bring their names and needs before the Lord of heaven and earth, our Father and Friend? What greater task could we have than to be a partner through prayer with God in His majestic work?

As good and beneficial as great preachers, doctors, missionaries, and statesmen can be, not all of us have been called to these tasks (God does have something vitally important He wants to do through you, though). There is one great task you *can* do—and you can do it right now. Come before His awesome throne and presence in prayer. It has been said that the greatest instrument Christ has in the world is a Christian who prays.

Will you be that mighty instrument?

Then do it!

▼